Percy Dearmer Revisited

Percy Dearmer Revisited

Discerning Authentically Anglican Liturgy
in a Multicultural, Ecumenical,
Twenty-First-Century Context

JARED C. CRAMER

WIPF & STOCK · Eugene, Oregon

PERCY DEARMER REVISITED
Discerning Authentically Anglican Liturgy in a Multicultural, Ecumenical, Twenty-First-Century Context

Copyright © 2020 Jared C. Cramer. All rights reserved. Except for brief quotations in critical publications or reviews, no part of this book may be reproduced in any manner without prior written permission from the publisher. Write: Permissions, Wipf and Stock Publishers, 199 W. 8th Ave., Suite 3, Eugene, OR 97401.

Wipf & Stock
An Imprint of Wipf and Stock Publishers
199 W. 8th Ave., Suite 3
Eugene, OR 97401

www.wipfandstock.com

PAPERBACK ISBN: 978-1-7252-7878-3
HARDCOVER ISBN: 978-1-7252-7879-0
EBOOK ISBN: 978-1-7252-7880-6

Manufactured in the U.S.A. 09/30/20

To the people of St. John's Episcopal Church
in Grand Haven, Michigan, who have showed me over this
past decade that the true beauty of Anglican liturgy is found
in the gathered people of God, united by our *Book of Common
Prayer*, and formed by our worship into a movement to bring
beauty and justice to a broken and hurting world.
Thank you for the gift of serving as your priest.

> I know perfectly well why I personally became a Christian. It was because I felt that the world is extremely beautiful, but eminently unsatisfactory.
>
> —Percy Dearmer

Contents

Acknowledgments		ix
Introduction		xiii
1	Percy Dearmer in Context	1
2	The Limitations of Dearmer's Work	23
3	An Anglican Approach, Neither Catholic Nor Protestant	36
4	The Ideals of English Liturgy	56
5	Conclusion—Dearmer Revisited	88
Bibliography		105
Index		111

Acknowledgments

GIVEN THE VARIETY OF liturgical styles, tastes, and approaches that exist in Christianity—and even within Anglicanism itself—to write a book that even attempts to present an "authentically Anglican approach" feels like a risky act. And while I am confident I do not have all the answers, I do believe Percy Dearmer offers us insight and direction. As I sought to articulate that insight in this work, I am deeply grateful to the several people who helped me in this project. Due to their assistance and guidance, I do hope that this book will be helpful to the average cleric, interested lay person, and seminarian who wants to be a part of creating liturgy that gives a true experience of God's beauty and goodness.

Much of the energy and insight for this book occurred while going through the Doctor of Ministry program at the School of Theology at the University of the South in Sewanee, TN. It was a robust, challenging, and tremendously formative experience over the course of several summers. I'm grateful to the work of the Rev. Dr. Benjamin King, Associate Professor of Church History, Director of the Advanced Degrees Program, and now the Academic Dean of Sewanee, who cultivated a program of doctoral-level continuing education that brought in professors of the highest caliber for a rigorous experience of study and praxis. I took every class I could with Dr. King and every single one was excellent. I have rarely known a professor of whom I can speak so highly.

Acknowledgments

Also, throughout my time at Sewanee, several professors provided helpful feedback on several parts of this present work. I'm grateful to the Rev. Canon Professor Mark Chapman, vice-principal and academic dean at Ripon College Cuddesdon, who helped me better understand the nuances of Anglican theology and history. I'm grateful to the Rt. Rev. J. Neil Alexander, former dean of the School of Theology, and the Rev. Dr. James F. Turrel, current dean of the School of Theology, for helping me understand the structure of ritual better, particularly as it relates to the rites of Christian initiation. Similarly, Bishop Alexander helped me in a later course, along with the Rev. Dr. Melissa M. Hartley, associate university chaplain at Sewanee, develop a stronger sense of liturgical time and how that influences the celebration of our liturgical rites.

In the end, of all of those professors, my strongest debts of gratitude goes to Dr. King and Dean Turrell, who served as readers for the first version of this work and who were tremendously helpful in the work of strengthening it so that it might be a helpful exploration of Dearmer. Dr. King's comment near the end that I had "won him over" on Dearmer made the whole experience entirely worth it. Their feedback in our final conversation proved helpful to the further revisions I have done to the manuscript to prepare it for publication to a broader audience.

As I worked though revising this into something suitable for broader publication, I'm grateful to the Rev. Robert Hart, now retired, who carefully read the manuscript and provided numerous points of suggested change and improvement. The fact that I write these acknowledgments on the Feast of St. Columba—a saint who means so much to Fr. Hart and upon whom I spent much time meditating during my retreat on the Isle of Iona before I came to take my current position at St. John's—will delight him to no end. The Spirit has a lovely way of bringing things full circle.

I also note my gratitude to Matthew Wimer, editorial production manager at Wipf and Stock, for his willingness to see this project come to publication. Editorial administrator George Callihan, copy editor Emily Callihan, copy editor Caleb Shupe, and typesetter Dr. Savanah N. Landerholm were all tremendously helpful at several points during the path of shepherding this through to

Acknowledgments

completion. Working with their publication company has been a lovely experience.

The final work of this project took place during the coronavirus pandemic, while our church building was closed and I worked from my home. It proved an interesting (and sometimes challenging!) experience to complete a book on the nature of Anglican liturgy and all her beauty while being cut off from the physical presence of my worshiping community. Though a recurrent refrain in recent years in the Episcopal Church has been that buildings do not matter, I know in a more acute way how much our sacred space is indeed important. True, Christians of all traditions have learned how to survive creatively during this time of global pandemic, but I believe we have also developed a renewed appreciation for the experience of grace in physical ways—the smell of a building, the way liturgical architecture brings you into an experience of the divine, the richness of vestments so often given in memory of someone who has died and who yet joins us at every Eucharistic celebration. I long for the beauty of Anglican worship, in all its fullness, and look forward to being able to return to that rich nourishing bedrock of our Christian life when it is safe to do so.

My gratitude to my own congregation of St. John's Episcopal Church has only been heightened by my physical absence from them in these past several months. Their willingness to take me as a rector at a young age and to stay with me over these past ten years has been one of the greatest gifts of my ordained life. They have a lovely space, work diligently to offer experiences of beautiful and faithful worship in the best of the Anglican worship, and are always hard at work bringing greater goodness and justice to the world around them. For these reasons, and so many more, it is to them that this book is dedicated.

Finally, during this time of pandemic, my wife, Bethany, and my daughter, Lucy, have been my "in-person" Christian community. The household is always the first locus of the Christian faith and practicing my faith with them these past several months has made me all the more grateful for the way Christ is present to me in each of them. Thank you, Bethany, for your patience and tender support as your husband always seems to find another project or

Acknowledgments

degree he wants to work on. Thank you, Lucy, for interrupting my work with requests for just one more kiss or hug when you should be napping. The deepest beauty of God's love and goodness is manifest to me in each of you. Though I do indeed resonate with Percy Dearmer's experience in the epigraph that begins this book that the world is both beautiful and unsatisfactory, I can say with all the joy I can muster that life with you is beyond satisfactory. It is exquisite.

Jared+

The Feast of St. Columba, Abbot of Iona †597

Introduction

IT MIGHT FAIRLY BE asked why one would turn to an Anglican liturgical scholar like Percy Dearmer (1867–1936) for insight into authentic Anglican liturgy in the twenty-first century. In particular, the question might be asked whether the goal of "authentic" Anglican liturgy is even worthwhile. For some, the idea of authentic Anglican liturgy simply sounds like trying to hone a certain Britishness in the style of liturgical celebration—an ideal which may have been lauded at one time, but which seems unhelpful in our contemporary context. For others, as long as the prayer book is somehow connected to worship, it would be argued that a service is an authentically Anglican experience of worship.

So, at the beginning, it is important to say that the goal of this work is not to convert people to the particular style of liturgy traced back to Dearmer and often called "English Use." Indeed, the idea that Dearmer's work can be summarized in the use of appareled amices, dorsal curtains, riddel posts, and other practices he encouraged is to miss the true scope and nature of his work. It is to miss the deep ideals which remained constant in the wide breadth of his writings.

The question of Dearmer's value is further complicated by the misguided perception that Dearmer's works exist primarily in a polemical nature. That is, Dearmer was only interested in fighting against Romanizing tendencies—and isn't that concept out-moded in an ecumenical age? The twentieth century saw a fundamental

INTRODUCTION

shift in the worship of the Christian church across denominations and traditions. A variety of streams, some reaching back as far as the sixteenth century, coalesced to form what would become known as the Liturgical Movement.[1] This movement brought together liturgical scholars from multiple denominations who were focused on the renewal of the worship of the church, particularly through the return to biblical and patristic sources. After Vatican II, and subsequent shifts in other Christian traditions, the worship of believers throughout Christianity became more unified in approach, structure, and principles. Given these changes, would not looking to Dearmer be looking in the wrong direction?

Perhaps so.

But I would suggest not. Rather, any good ecumenist will tell you that ecumenical dialogue is best furthered not by simply wiping away the peculiarities of each tradition, but instead by deeper understanding and appreciation of one's own tradition. Only with such an understanding can we intelligently and thoughtfully interact with the traditions of others. This is true just as much in the area of liturgy as it is in the areas of history and theology.

So, while it is certain that some readers will come to the idea of looking to Dearmer for insight into the ideals of Anglican liturgy with a healthy amount of skepticism, I would encourage such skepticism to be held lightly. One of the hallmarks of the Anglican tradition is its generosity, its attempt to be an embracing approach that invites catholic and protestant together in a united act of worship. This path is often described as a *via media* but I have elsewhere referred to as a *via amplectens*, an embracing way that draws together both catholic and protestant streams.[2] And though Dearmer's work has certainly resulted in a particular style of worship for one part of the church, his underlying ideals for worship in the Anglican tradition are able to function in many of the wide variety of pieties and liturgical practices that exist in the Anglican Communion. Truly, his ideals articulate a unifying approach to worship that is at once thoroughly Anglican in nature and also instructive for any

---

1. For a description of the roots behind the movement, see Fenwick and Spinks, *Worship in Transition*, 13–21.

2. Cramer, *Safeguarded by Glory*, 35.

INTRODUCTION

Christian who wishes to explore these Anglican principles and how they might deepen worship in any tradition.

Though names like John Mason Neale (1818–66), W. H. Frere (1863–1938), and Massey Shepherd (1913–90) are more well-known when it comes to central figures in the development of Anglican liturgy, Percy Dearmer also had a significant impact upon the worship life of the Anglican Communion. As one scholar notes,

> He, more than anyone else, perceived the extent to which [the worship of the church] had become impoverished through unimaginative and often careless ordering of services in parish churches and cathedrals, the failure to grasp the importance of good music, and the readiness to accept the dreary and ugly in the setting of worship.[3]

Dearmer operated at a time when the heat of the Ritualist controversy was finally beginning to die down and he was, thus, able to engage that movement critically, particularly placing it within the context of late nineteenth- and early twentieth-century Anglican worship. It must be remembered that the early shape of the Liturgical Movement in England was mediated through the leaders of the Ritualists—alongside of the leaders in the Christian Socialist Movement.[4] Dearmer brought together both streams and created something new, an "English Use" approach to liturgy.

His approach was not widely affirmed when *The Parson's Handbook* was first published. As Walter Matthews notes, his originality "was not always understood or relished by people of cautious minds."[5] Yet Dearmer continued to work and hone his understanding of what good Anglican liturgy should look like. "As he himself has said, he did not stop thinking at the age of forty-five, and he was never a purveyor of clichés and settled opinions."[6] We see this throughout the twelve editions he wrote of *The Parson's Handbook*. He was never settled that he had gotten it right—or that, if he had, it

---

3. Beeson, "Master of Ceremonies," 99.
4. See the argument made for these two key sources in Fenwick and Spinks, *Worship in Transition*, 39–40.
5. Matthews, "Introduction," 13.
6. Matthews, "Introduction," 13.

should not be looked at slightly differently given changes in church and society.

Thus, this seems to be a particularly appropriate time for a reappraisal of the work of Percy Dearmer. In the pages that follow, his work will be examined in context with both the man himself and also the times in which he lived. Some time will be spent evaluating the limitations of Dearmer's work, not only when it comes to the scope of this particular project, but also due to the cultural and historical limitations of the time in which he wrote. Next, there will be a sketching of what his "English Use" approach to liturgy actually consists of. Through this study, key ideals for Anglican liturgy will be discerned, tested, and then explored for how they might make the worship of Anglicans today ever more faithful, beautiful, authentic, and true.

1

Percy Dearmer in Context

THE NINETEENTH CENTURY WAS a time of significant development in Anglican Christianity. As leaders in the Oxford Movement argued for their own reinterpretation of Anglican history, tracing a version of Anglican Catholic Christianity through history, others asserted a different view based upon the importance of changes during the Reformation.[1]

Though much of Dearmer's work focused on art, architecture, and liturgy, these interests came from two important streams of late nineteenth-century English Christianity: the Ritualists and the developing Christian Socialist Movement. Dearmer first engaged both of these while a student at Christ Church, Oxford, through his experience with two people: Thomas Banks Strong and York Powell. Strong, who later became Dean of Christ Church, then Bishop

1. Much of the content that follows in this chapter is based upon an earlier paper written for Mark Chapman in "Anglican Theology" during the Advanced Degrees Program at the School of Theology of the University of the South, August 15, 2012. Other content throughout the book related to the Sarum Use and also to the history of baptism in the British Isles is adapted and reworked from an earlier paper written for J. Neil Alexander and James F. Turrell in "Mapping Liturgical Structures" during the Advanced Degrees Program at the School of Theology of the University of the South, August 10, 2013. For an exploration of the nineteenth-century reinterpretation of the Reformation, see Chapman, *Anglican Theology*.

of Ripon, followed by Oxford, introduced Dearmer "to a style of churchmanship which would certainly not have been approved by his Evangelical school-teacher mother."[2] Powell, who described himself as a "decent heathen Aryan," introduced Dearmer to socialism. As Gray notes, "At Oxford, the art master's son began to realize that there were social, political, and religious implications behind his natural instinct to celebrate beauty. Powell emphasized the social and political, Strong taught him about the religious."[3] Dearmer was certainly not the first Anglican to connect a high approach to worship with an emphasis upon the social implications of Christianity. Indeed, as will be argued below, Dearmer stands squarely in the stream of the Christian Socialist Movement in the Anglican tradition. As we will see, these two streams—Ritualism and Christian Socialism—exercised significant influence over the broad shape of his work and thought.

It was in the context of these two formative streams of thought that Dearmer was ordained in 1891. By that time, the ecclesial and liturgical debates of the nineteenth century continued, but had begun to mature, shift, and change, cooling in their tenor and their force. This created an ecclesial culture wherein the articulation of what constituted Anglicanism remained immensely important but was less violently debated. Some of this was because the church had begun to self-segregate into various microclimates of practice and belief. However, the lessening of fierce debate was also because aspects of the various parties of churchmanship had begun to be accepted by large numbers within the culture.

Thus, during Dearmer's time, the Ritualists and Evangelicals still waged in battle. Yet, many churches had, in practice, affirmed a higher approach to worship as vestments and other ornaments became less problematic. At the same time, the majority of Anglicans still embraced the evangelical rejection of all things Roman. Both the development of the Ritualist Movement alongside the parallel development of Christian Socialism worked together to form Dearmer.

---

2. Gray, "British Museum Religion," 4.
3. Gray, "British Museum Religion," 4.

Thus, both the development in approaches to worship in Anglican Christianity in his time and the parallel growth of Christian Socialism are fundamental to understanding why his work was much more than so-called "British Museum Religion." At the same time, these social contexts do not fully explain the forces that guided Dearmer in his life and ministry. A brief look at his early life and upbringing will also give clues and perspective to the ideals he later articulated in his writings.

BIOGRAPHICAL INFLUENCES ON PERCY DEARMER'S THOUGHT[4]

On February 27, 1867, Percy Dearmer was born in Kilburn, Middlesex, to Thomas Dearmer (a bank clerk who quit his career to become a painter) and Caroline Miriam Turner (the owner of a girls' school, Somerset House). Thomas was an artist and musician who used to gather friends to play and was also a personal friend of Charles Dickens. Throughout his life he would travel and paint, particularly watercolors. Suffice it to say, Percy grew up with art all around him—a reality that would deeply influence his later approaches to liturgy and Christianity as a whole.

Thomas met Percy's mother, Caroline, when he went to teach a drawing class at the school she owned. Two years after he started teaching, they married. However, Percy did not remember their marriage as a happy one. In the words of Percy's second wife, Nan, "Percy retained no gentle memories of [his mother], only harsh ones."[5] As a child, Percy would dread his parents' frequent fights, as Caroline disapproved of the more leisurely life Thomas led. Thomas died when Percy was ten years old, and the rest of his upbringing with his mother was filled with more difficult memories. Dearmer's wife, Nan, believed that he (Percy) was a sensitive child and that his mother, Caroline, favored Percy's elder brother, Edgar. Even later in

---

4. Much of this section is drawn from material found throughout the biography written by his second wife, Nan, in Dearmer, *Life of Percy Dearmer*. Citations will only be used in this section when quoting directly from the work.

5. Dearmer, *Life of Percy Dearmer*, 25–26.

life, Percy retained a "cold dislike" for her.[6] She sought to push her evangelical beliefs on Percy, but he consistently resisted them, refusing even to accompany her to Spurgeon's Tabernacle. This perhaps makes it clear why he never was attracted later in life to the arguments or practices of more evangelical Anglicans. As his mother's attention increasingly focused on Edgar and his weak health, Percy found new love in the art museums of London, carefully studying and learning about architecture, furnishings, glass, ivories, and pottery. The seeds were being planted for his later career.

It was during this period that his tutor, York Powell, introduced him to the work of John Ruskin and William Morris, leading to the arousal of his interest in the social implications of art.[7] As Dearmer was concluding his time at Oxford, he went from an earlier interest in architecture to a sense of calling to Holy Orders. When his mother refused to support his formation for ordained ministry, he discovered his father had left him a small inheritance. The remainder of the cost of his training was covered by working as a secretary for Charles Gore at Pusey House in Oxford. Working closely with Gore throughout his training meant that when time came for ordination, he was a thoroughly formed high churchman with strong views on social justice. Indeed, while working in his first several positions, his superiors often complained to the bishop that Dearmer was neglecting parish responsibilities because of his significant social justice involvements.

In addition to frustrations with Dearmer's commitments to social justice work, his time devoted to writing and his interest in liturgy was another source of friction with superiors. The bishop who ordained Dearmer—Randall Davidson, who went on to be the longest-serving Archbishop of Canterbury since the Reformation—never thought Dearmer could be a model parish priest because he simply could not understand how a priest could believe God cared about color, ceremony, and poetry. As Harold Anson recalled, "I tried more than once to interpret Dearmer to the great Archbishop but I am sure he always thought of him as a rather effeminate man,

---

6. Dearmer, *Life of Percy Dearmer*, 28.
7. Beeson, "Master of Ceremonies," 101.

who was more interested in colours than commentaries, and preferred writing to house visiting."[8]

Early in Dearmer's career, while serving at St. Anne's, South Lambeth, he struggled fitting into the ideals of parish ministry. He had married Mabel Jessie Pritchard White, a friend of many years with whom he rather rapidly and unexpectedly fell in love. He was twenty-four and she was nineteen. Dearmer's mother thought the marriage was a foolish idea, that Mabel would only encourage him to continue to pursue the political and aesthetic interests he loved. She was, of course, entirely correct in that respect. Mabel's works as an author of children's books and plays survive as testament to the rich artistry in their home. The young couple both loved things of beauty and had strong socialist political beliefs. This made life a challenge as a young priest and they both struggled to live the life they desired. His vicar at St. Anne's, W. A. Morrris, was increasingly frustrated by the time his assistant curate—still only in his mid-twenties—was spending lecturing on socialism, working for the Christian Social Union, and writing for journals and other outlets. At the end of 1893, Morris wrote to the Bishop of Rochester, insisting that it was time for Dearmer either to give up his work for the Christian Social Union and his literary efforts or to leave the parish. Morris wanted to have a curate who could truly help him in his work caring for a parish with a population of ten thousand in the community. He had affection for Dearmer, but the working relationship had become untenable.[9]

From St. Anne's, Dearmer went on to serve St. John's, Great Marlborough Street, in the Diocese of London. From the very beginning, the parish agreed that he would only work part-time as a curate so that he could devote the rest of the time to journalism and speaking on behalf of the Christian Social Union. In addition to a better working arrangement, he and Mabel much preferred the life of London to that of their previous home.[10]

---

8. Gray, *Percy Dearmer*, 26–27.
9. Gray, *Percy Dearmer*, 26–31.
10. Gray, *Percy Dearmer*, 31–33.

After several years, during which he made friends and even saw his old mentor Charles Gore appointed a Canon of Westminster, he was offered the position of assistant to the priest-in-charge of Berkeley Chapel in 1897. Berkeley was what is known in the Church of England as a proprietary chapel—that is, it is supported by private individuals and has no official ecclesial constitutional existence or parochial rights. Though many proprietary chapels were focused on extreme Evangelical churchmanship, the worship at Berkeley was dignified and the music was for many years led by Henry Briggs, an expert in plainsong chant. It was at Berkeley that Dearmer first tried his hand at catechism instruction for children, something, it turned out, for which he had quite a skill.[11]

After a short year at Berkeley, the Dearmers moved again so he could take up the role of curate at St. Mark's, Marylebone Road, under the leadership of its vicar, Morris Fuller. Under Fuller's leadership, the worship at St. Mark's had developed an elaborate ceremonial based on the Roman Rite. However, by the time Dearmer came to St. Mark's, Fuller was increasingly ill and absent and so Dearmer took the opportunity to shape things according to his own temperament—one that was still high church in style but that eschewed imitation of the practices of the Roman Catholics. He made his own views on the question of liturgy clear in 1899, when he published the first edition of *The Parson's Handbook*. It quickly became a bestseller in the Church of England—even though Dearmer had yet to hold the position of vicar in a parish.[12]

Two years after the publication of *The Parson's Handbook*, Dearmer received his first incumbent post—the position of Vicar at St. Mary's, Primrose Hill. St. Mary's was a young congregation. Dearmer was only their third vicar. The congregation had been connected with Christian Socialism from the start. The first vicar, Charles James Fuller, was a Tractarian and led worship in the High Church style with decidedly Catholic approaches to teaching. As Gray notes,

11. Gray, *Percy Dearmer*, 35.

12. Gray, *Percy Dearmer*, 35. See also Dearmer, *Life of Percy Dearmer*, 98–103.

St. Mary's became alive with the conviction that the Catholic faith was something that must play its full part in every aspect of daily life, and not be limited to the narrow confines of Sunday worship only. Not only were the sacraments duly administered, but also the wants of the needy were relieved, injustices righted and ignorance dispelled.[13]

Fuller was threatened with legal action by the Bishop of London under the Public Worship Regulation Act, which caused him to scale down his more elaborate ceremonial. However, when Frederick Temple became Bishop of London, this approach was reversed and the high approach to liturgy was able to resume.[14]

When Dearmer took the position in 1901, the parish was healthy, financially strong, and secure in the high church tradition. However, he wasted no time in adjusting the worship to be more in keeping with the ideals of *The Parson's Handbook*. It was claimed that one of his first actions was to dispose of the six candlesticks on the high altar and burn them in the church furnace—a rather unlikely action, but one that conveys the perception of many as to just how committed he was to seeing the ideals of *The Parson's Handbook* put into place. He lime-washed the interior, beginning with the vault, walls of the chancel, and the side chapel. He introduced side curtains on either side of the altar, lowered the reredos to a height he thought was more fitting to the proportions of the church, and lengthened the altar itself. Dearmer himself would confess later he made some of his first changes too quickly—but as many clergy (including myself!) can tell you from experience, this is not uncommon for your first incumbent position as a priest. However, he began to see the ideals of his handbook in practice, along with his equally important goals of advancing the social witness of the church and an increased interest in improving the quality of church music.[15]

One more item of note in his personal life was the tragedy which befell him after he had spent ten years at St. Mary's, Primrose

---

13. Gray, *Percy Dearmer*, 58.
14. Gray, *Percy Dearmer*, 57–59.
15. Gray, *Percy Dearmer*, 59–60.

Hill, as vicar. He was beginning to feel at a loss in the parish, that he had done what he could, and was yearning for something more. So, when the first World War broke out, he decided to serve as a priest to the nursing units in Serbia. His wife Mabel went with him to work as a nurse. However, she was struck down by enteric fever. He returned to St. Mary's, devastated, and only three months later was given the report that their son, Christopher, had been killed in the Dardanelles. This double personal tragedy, alongside the national pain from the first World War, deeply impacted the rest of his life as a priest and author. It explains, perhaps, the constant tension he felt between the desire to do something more for the larger church and yet his belief that parochial ministry was the place where a priest's life could best be served. He simply no longer found a calling for himself in parish life.

Dearmer resigned from St. Mary's and began to travel, preach, and lecture. He never held another living as a priest. During this time, he met and married his second wife, Nancy Knowles—more fondly known as Nan—in a small quiet ceremony at which William Temple was the officiant. Alongside of them, Nan's biography of Percy became an important (though, naturally, somewhat hagiographic) source to all who studied his life and ministry.

Truth be told, it seems a slight pain and melancholy had followed him throughout life, from childhood until his twilight years. Though his book had been successful, and he had influenced countless clergy in the Church of England, Dearmer was not fully recognized by the larger church until near the end of his life, when he was appointed a canon at Westminster Abbey. His appointment was opposed by the dean, William Foxley Norris,[16] but he served in the role for the final five years of his life, the first four years of work being particularly significant in raising the liturgical standards at the Abbey. He died suddenly in the spring of 1936, at the age of sixty-nine, working on yet another book that would be published posthumously, *Man and His Maker*.[17]

---

16. Dearmer, *Life of Percy Dearmer*, 99.
17. Dearmer, *Life of Percy Dearmer*, 111.

This brief sketch of Dearmer's life demonstrates his passion for art, his commitment to social justice, and his strong concerns for the worship life of the average parish. One also gets a sense that he never felt he truly found a place to settle—other than his tenure at St. Mary's—and always felt a little out of place in the church he loved. Given the impact he had upon the church—not only in the area of liturgy, but also in the area of music—it is sad that official recognition from the church was so long in coming. However, two of the most significant drivers in his work merit further exploration to get at the root of what he would produce in his life. The first is the role of the Tractarian and Ritualist Movements and the second is the role of Christian Socialism.

THE TRACTARIANS AND THE RITUALIST MOVEMENT

Two movements in the nineteenth century had a profound impact upon the life of the Church of England: the Oxford Movement and the Ritualists. Though often placed together as a single stream, they must be seen as related—and yet distinct—developments. Each must be examined in turn, as both had distinct influences on Dearmer's approach to the worship of the church. Further, the High Church antecedents to these movements must also be considered in order to gather a full understanding of the context of late nineteenth-century Anglican Christianity.

The early nineteenth-century Oxford Movement (whose followers are often called Tractarians, after the *Tracts for Our Times*) arose in response to many forces present in the Church of England. Evangelicalism was on the rise, as was theological liberalism. There was also the decreasing influence of the Church of England upon British society and, in particular, the state's increasing hesitance to support the church as traditionally understood.[18] Here the Oxford Movement was a development from the High Churchmen of previous generations who had battled against the Erastian Low

18. Chapman, *Anglicanism*, 75. For a fuller explanation of this reality, see 75–86.

Churchmen of their own time.[19] Indeed, though the political origins of the beginning of the Oxford Movement are often overlooked, they represent a key connection between the early Tractarians and the old High Church party.[20]

As disappointment with the monarch and frustration with civil government grew, however, the political approach of the Oxford Movement turned to one that argued for an even higher view of the church with respect to government, "Froude's church–state ideal was not the constitutionalism of Hooker or even the Laudian theocracy of the Caroline Divines. Rather, it found its model exemplified by that unqualified ecclesiastical supremacy over the civil power in all capacities, symbolized by Becket and the twelfth-century church dictating to monarchs."[21] That is, the High Church and anti-Erastian views of Oxford Movement leaders led often to an anti-state and anti-establishment perspective on English life.

The theological ground of the Oxford Movement focused on a return to the Church Fathers and antiquity. But here, once more, they deviated from the older High Church view. Older High churchmen had seen the Fathers as evidence for the rightness of the doctrine of the Church of England following the Reformation. The Tractarians, however, believed that the Church Fathers were the absolute source and authority for church teaching. In seeking to follow their understanding of the early church, the Tractarians were increasingly comfortable disregarding the teachings and views of not only English Reformers but also the modern episcopate as it existed in their own time—another key differentiation between them and the classical High Church tradition.[22]

Two principles which guided the Tractarians were Reserve and Economy. As explained by Herring, "Reserve was the withholding of sacred truths as too precious to be revealed to the uninitiated or antagonistic, while Economy was setting out those truths to their best advantage by teaching them only at a speed or in a manner

19. For background of this struggle, see Chamberlain, *Accommodating High Churchmen*, 22–28.

20. Nockles, *Oxford Movement in Context*, 67–72.

21. Nockles, *Oxford Movement in Context*, 81.

22. Nockles, *Oxford Movement in Context*, 113–21.

Percy Dearmer in Context

in which their content could be properly understood by groups or individuals."[23] Thus, when it came to ritual practice, the Tractarians were much more restrained than the Ritualists who followed them. As Pusey once explained, "We felt it was very much easier to change a dress than to change the heart, and that externals might be gained at the cost of the doctrines themselves."[24] These principles of Reserve and Economy created a practice of moderation in parochial work, particularly with regard to worship.

In addition to these two key principles, Tractarianism can be understood as including several key concepts. There was a strong resistance among practitioners of Tractarianism to Romanizing just as much as to Protestantism. As Herring notes, "For the mainstream of *via media* Tractarians the disaster [when several Church of England clergy converted to Rome] was not the losing of the Romanizers but to have acquired them in the first place."[25] The relationship of the people and their priest was essential,[26] with clergy being urged to be sensitive to the needs, experiences, and caution of their parishioners.[27] This was founded upon the Tractarian principal of Economy, "They remained deeply reluctant to move without giving the necessary instruction to, and obtaining the consent of, their most significant parishioners."[28] There was a strong rejection of the common practice of doing things cheaply instead of well.[29] There was also an ideal of calling the people back to the ideals of the *Book of Common Prayer*, believing it was "a primary source of authority" and using it regularly as a tool in teaching.[30]

To be clear, the approach to worship in the Oxford Movement was indeed higher than other contemporary Anglicans. However, the underlying principle was not the ceremonial itself, it was the

23. Herring, *Oxford Movement in Practice*, 12.
24. Liddon, *Life of Pusey*, 4:212–13, cited by Nockles, *Oxford Movement in Context*, 213.
25. Herring, *Oxford Movement in Practice*, 36.
26. Herring, *Oxford Movement in Practice*, 71.
27. Herring, *Oxford Movement in Practice*, 103.
28. Herring, *Oxford Movement in Practice*, 215.
29. Herring, *Oxford Movement in Practice*, 98.
30. Herring, *Oxford Movement in Practice*, 158.

focus and devotion of the congregations. As W. E. Heygate argued, the difference between Evangelical parishes and Tractarian parishes "is not a better decorated church, nor chanting, nor rubrical exactness, nor anything of the sort in which that vital difference consists; but *it is something in principle which causes this great difference in practice*, that there is a better informed piety, a more frequent and devout worship, a reverent and quiet spirit, a more liberal charity, a more disciplined life."[31] It was these latter ideals which occupied the energy of the Tractarians. Changes in ceremonial were on the periphery of their concerns, only intended to arise after the heart and mind of the people had been sufficiently turned and then trained.

In the years following 1860, however, a different movement arose in the Church of England: Ritualism. Initially, many Tractarian leaders were sympathetic (publicly at least) to the Ritualists, believing they were often unfairly persecuted. However, as Ritualism grew it became clear that its principles were significantly out of step with those of early Tractarian Anglicanism. Though the great Tractarian, John Henry Newman himself, had once written, "Give us more services, more vestments and decorations in worship," the Tractarians did so through the importation of Roman practices. Newman strongly rejected this approach in an 1849 letter, writing, "When you propose to return to *lost* Church of England ways you are rational, but when you invent *new* ceremonial which never was, when you copy Roman or other foreign rituals, you are neither respectable nor rational."[32]

The Tractarians did not believe the prayer book was perfect, but they were very concerned with the work of putting it into practice "as they found it."[33] The Ritualist approach ran very counter to Tractarians. They had a tendency to disregard the prayer book, believing "the rules of the *Book of Common Prayer* are not to be understood in their natural sense, but only as they are interpreted by the Roman ordinal; that, in fact, the *Book of Common Prayer*

---

31. Herring, *Oxford Movement in Practice*, 40.
32. Cited by Herring, *Oxford Movement in Practice*, 193.
33. Herring, *Oxford Movement in Practice*, 208.

is merely an imperfect or emasculated missal."[34] Indeed, both with regard to the prayer book and the church in general, to the Tractarians the Ritualists were just another type of nonconformist.[35] Pusey warned Ritualist clergy about the danger of being "Presbyterian toward their bishops and Popes toward their people."[36]

At the same time, despite the controversy, both the Oxford Movement (and later, the Ritualists) had significant impact upon the Church of England. Spencer notes that though they likely never made up more than 5 percent of the total clergy from 1841 to 1871, "By the beginning of the twentieth century, eastward facing celebration, weekly communion and candles on the altar had become the norm, with a widespread acceptance of vestments."[37] Of Spencer's identifying characteristics, weekly communion was indeed a goal of Tractarianism, but the rest are more accurately those of Ritualist clergy whose focus was specifically on candles, vestments, and an advocacy of eastward facing that was stronger than Tractarian practice.[38] And yet, it would be a mistake to take the common use of these outward practices as a mark of success either for the Oxford Movement or the Tractarians. For both groups, the inward beliefs were just as important. Tractarians would want to know if the faith and spirituality, the hold on Christian truth, was stronger in their parishioners. The adoption of what had been seen as Ritualist practices without a similar change in theological belief would have made no sense.[39]

---

34. Herring, *Oxford Movement in Practice*, 223.

35. Herring, *Oxford Movement in Practice*, 234.

36. Herring, *Oxford Movement in Practice*, 218.

37. Spencer, *SCM Studyguide to Anglicanism*, 126. Chapman also notes this reality, including how this did not mean Anglo-Catholic had become particularly popular: "Although the extraordinary achievement of the ritualists had left virtually no church building untouched by the Gothic revival, which meant that worship, even in country parishes, was almost unrecognizably different from 70 years before, most Church of England people and clergy would have been reluctant to identify themselves as Anglo-Catholic." Chapman, *Anglicanism*, 88.

38. Herring, *Oxford Movement in Practice*, 190–93.

39. Herring, *Oxford Movement in Practice*, 246–48.

Percy Dearmer Revisited

In Dearmer's time, the controversies of both the Oxford Movement and the Tractarians had certainly lessened in fervor. Once controversial practices were becoming more common. Though Dearmer was suspicious of some aspects of the Ritualist Movement,[40] in the end he believed that history had put the Ritualists in a difficult spot. In Dearmer's mind, many of the bishops did not have sufficient understanding of the rubrics of the *Book of Common Prayer*. "Consequently, 'ritualistic' clergy were sometimes forced to disobey the Bishops in order that they might obey the Prayer Book."[41] However, as time continued, Dearmer believed that this original necessity turned into a willful denial of the rubrics of the *Book of Common Prayer*, "in favour of the customs of a very hostile foreign church."[42] It was this willful disregard for the rubrics that led to his desire to articulate a catholic understanding of English worship that was still in line with the history, tradition, and ideals of the Church of England—an approach that was a return to earlier Tractarian ideals.

Indeed, though Dearmer advocated for the use of vestments, candles, and other parts of worship that typified Ritualism, though he engaged in similar legal and historical arguments about the Ornaments Rubric, he was clearly not a Ritualist. Rather, his work was an attempt to offer an alternative to the Ritualism of his time. Several of his own ideals identified in this work can be traced to the old Tractarian principles of Economy and Reserve. His departure from Ritualists on the subject of incense and the multiplicity of candles, his insistence upon attention to the prayer book, his insistence that the outward was incomplete without training on the inward truths of theology and spirituality—all of this came clearly from the Tractarian movement.

It should also be noted that when the Oxford or Ritualist movements did stray into more extreme and narrowly held convictions, it was often because of the passion of its adherents rather than the

---

40. Indeed, when referring to the ritualists in the preface to *The Parson's Handbook*, he makes a now oft-quoted comment, "Would that they always deserved the name!" Dearmer, *Parson's Handbook* (12th ed.), 3.

41. Dearmer, *Parson's Handbook* (12th ed.), 3.

42. Dearmer, *Parson's Handbook* (12th ed.), 3.

teaching of its leaders. For example, the practice of fasting before communion—though common among many Tractarians—was not one its leaders would have required of all faithful Christians. When arguing against the universal insistence on this practice, Dearmer quotes Edward Bouverie Pusey, a leader of the Oxford movement. Dearmer noted that though Pusey believed that fasting communion was a good custom for those who chose it, "There is no irreverence in non-fasting Communion. There is no binding law."[43] In this and other areas, there was a desire for a sense of moderation in the leaders of the movement—even if that moderation was not always maintained in the movement's adherents.

As the catholic wing of the Church of England developed and matured in the late nineteenth century, the theological underpinnings of what had once been understood as Ritualist worship were also beginning to be articulated. A significant part of this was found in the work of the Guild of St. Matthew, founded in 1877 by Stewart Headlam, the curate at St. Matthew's, Bethnal Green. Though he certainly was a part of the "High Church" party, for him it went beyond questions of Ritualism. For Headlam, "The vision displayed in the full ceremonial richness of Catholic worship should be allowed to deepen the mystery of the word made flesh—that which was incarnate at Bethlehem and now present in the faithful through Communion."[44] In particular, Headlam helped draw together the incarnational theme of worship with a strong emphasis upon sacraments and the social justice implications of Christianity—in that order. "We are socialists because we are sacramentalists," he insisted.[45] Their theology was becoming more concerned with questions of the incarnation and less with a particular argument for the relationship between the episcopate and the state or even an exclusive focus on ritual practice.

Much of this is eventually seen in the *Lux Mundi* movement, as several disciples of the early Tractarians began centering their thinking around the doctrine of the incarnation. When *Lux Mundi:*

43. Dearmer, *Truth about Fasting*, 114.
44. Gray, *Percy Dearmer*, 18.
45. Rowell, *Vision Glorious*, 240.

A Series of Studies in the Religion of the Incarnation was published in 1899, several theologians contributed to the work. The editor of the book was Charles Gore—the scholar for whom Dearmer had worked as a secretary. Indeed, *Lux Mundi* was published while Dearmer was still a student at Oxford, suggesting that he was familiar with the work in which Gore was engaged. In an essay from the volume written by the Sub-Warden (at the time) of Keble College, we read, "Hence this act of Eucharistic worship, above all others, has become the centre of unity. In it the church has offered its best to God: all the more external gifts of art, such as architecture, painting, and music, have been consecrated in worship."[46] Thus, the maturing of thought now connects sacramental worship with the incarnation, binding it all up with a calling that the theology behind this worship requires that we offer to God our very best. Key to this new generation of Anglo-Catholics, led by Gore, was that one could draw from the catholic tradition of the church without turning to Rome for validity and direction. All of this theological deepening would soon pervade much of Dearmer's own work with regard to liturgy and theology, with the incarnation and social justice playing a central theme.

When Dearmer published *The Parson's Handbook*, many of the controversial aspects of earlier Ritualism had begun to subside. This meant that people were more willing to consider deeper questions about the shape and nature of their worship apart from party allegiances. As Gray notes, "Many of the inhibitions about what was 'High' and 'Low' were beginning to disappear and a consensus was being reached which was able to accept an enhanced visual element in churches which only a few years earlier would have been quite unthinkable."[47] That is not to say that all approaches became acceptable. Many in the Church of England remained largely suspicious of anything that seemed too "Roman Catholic," making Dearmer's case for an "English Use" support of high worship rather attractive. The time was ripe for a new way of understanding and putting into practice the catholic heritage of the Church of England.

---

46. Lock, "Church," 392.
47. Gray, *Percy Dearmer*, 56.

CHRISTIAN SOCIALISM

Though it was originally through an atheistic socialist (Powell) that Dearmer was introduced to a leftist approach to politics, it was the development of explicitly Christian Socialism that had the greatest impact upon his work. The first book he published was actually not *The Parson's Handbook*, but *Christian Socialism and Practical Christianity*.[48] The teachings and emphases of Christian Socialism always played a strong role in all areas of this thought, liturgy and worship included.

Christian Socialism developed in the nineteenth century as a liberal approach to British social welfare continued to grow. In the 1850s and 1860s, F. D. Maurice wrote, articulating a vision of socialism that was "a cooperative order of society wherein all labored for the common good rather than private gain."[49] It was avowedly Christian Socialism for Maurice and others because they believed it was founded upon the teachings of Jesus and the New Testament. "Socialists were not fighting for a new system of their own devising, but for God's established order against the new competitive world which man's selfishness had created."[50] Christian Socialists believed they were recovering the heart of Jesus' teaching over and against the sinful tendencies of modern capitalism.

At first, Dearmer was significantly involved in Headlam's aforementioned Guild of St. Matthew. However, he eventually found himself drawn more to the work of the Christian Social Union (CSU), due to its more moderate and comprehensive objectives. Gore was president of the CSU and scholars believe it was through Dearmer's earlier time as a secretary for Gore that Dearmer "acquired his Maurician sympathies."[51] Unlike his previous

48. Dearmer, *Christian Socialism and Practical Christianity*.
49. Gray, *Percy Dearmer*, 17.
50. Gray, *Percy Dearmer*, 17.
51. Knight, *Victorian Christianity at the Fin de Siècle*, 128. Later in life, Gore and Dearmer experienced a falling out when Gore objected to Dearmer's work on the *English Hymnal*. As a former student of Gore, "Dearmer was deeply distressed by this, and he himself moved in the opposite direction, quietly dropping his Anglo-Catholicism in favour of thoroughgoing Anglican modernism." Knight, *Victorian Christianity at the Fin de Siècle*, 231.

engagement with the Guild of St. Matthew, the CSU did not identify solely with one political party. Instead, its members "might hold any political and economic theories they liked—as long as they allowed the Christian law to govern their social practice."[52] Dearmer was part of the founding of the CSU and was appointed a member of its executive committee.

The influence of Tractarianism, the results of Ritualism, and Dearmer's experience of Christian Socialism blended together to create a very particular approach to Christian worship, one that combined retrieval of English catholicism with the aesthetics of worship and the ethical questions surrounding the practice of worship. His insistence upon well-made and tasteful ornaments in worship was not, as many have supposed, mere fussiness. "For vulgarity, Dearmer explained, in the long run always means cheapness 'and cheapness means the tyranny of the sweaters [those who ran sweatshops].'"[53] Dearmer would go on,

> A modern preacher often stands in a sweated pulpit, wearing a sweated surplice over a suit of clothes that were not produced under fair conditions, and, holding a sweated book in one hand, with the other he points to the machine-made cross on the jerry-built altar, and appeals to the sacred principles of mutual sacrifice and love.[54]

His concern for the poor was inextricable from his concern for beauty. Indeed, he believed they were one and the same and were based squarely upon the importance of the gospel of Christ.

Furthermore, the ideals of Christian Socialism, for Dearmer, meant more than changing an unjust economic system to favor the poor and oppressed. "It meant opening the kingdom of art and

---

52. Gray, "British Museum Religion," 7.

53. Gray, "British Museum Religion," 7.

54. As cited by Gray, "British Museum Religion," 11. In Dearmer's opinion, this situation had improved by the publishing of the twelfth edition of *The Parson's Handbook*. However, the better produced ornaments are still problematic for him as they were at that point being used to replace older and, one assumes, more beautiful originals. Dearmer, *Parson's Handbook* (12th ed.), 4–5.

Percy Dearmer in Context

beauty to all."[55] This had been a foundational belief of others in the Ritualist Movement as well, "The richness of Eucharistic worship was not only the legitimate heritage of the Church of England, but that which embodied as nothing else could the sense of the reality of Divine grace in a way which could be grasped by the poor and unlettered."[56] Dearmer then set out to craft an approach to liturgy that paid attention to the best of these influences while still searching for the elusive goal of authentic Anglican practice.

"BRITISH MUSEUM RELIGION"

With these concerns in mind, Dearmer dove deep within the resources of the British Library, seeking to retrieve what might be an authentically Anglican approach to liturgical questions. It was this method, however, which created the oft-repeated charge of "British Museum Religion." Indeed, the only engagement with Dearmer mustered by many scholars (particularly those of recent years, with the exception, of course, of Donald Gray), is by using that phrase as a way of dismissing his work, as though that is all that needs to be said.

The phrase itself was coined by James Adderly, who worked with Dearmer at Berkeley Chapel in Mayfair.[57] It was during this time that Dearmer was spending much time at the British Museum researching for *The Parson's Handbook*—thus the phrase does have a rather literal genesis. Adderly himself did not necessarily believe this phrase meant Dearmer's work should be disregarded. Instead he insisted that Dearmer was "just the man to rescue liturgiology from the pedantry of the mere man of letters and make it attractive

---

55. Gray, *Percy Dearmer*, 20.

56. Rowell, *Vision Glorious*, 117.

57. In his 1916 book, *In Slums and Society*, Adderly acknowledges that others might claim inspiration for this phrase, but insists that he was the first to use it. It was a time of great upheaval in liturgical practice, and Adderly says that he was the one who got Dearmer thinking along what became his fundamental question by continually asking him, "Is this in the Prayer Book?" Cited by Dearmer, *Life of Percy Dearmer*, 103.

to the whole church."[58] Furthermore, the idea that he spent his time primarily consulting the Sarum missal and looking at plates of medieval worship is far from the truth. As Gray notes, as early as 1899 he was engaging constructively with the work of two other key Anglican liturgical scholars of his time.[59] He expressed appreciation for the suggestions and changes of both Frank Edward Brightman[60] and Walter Howard Frere.[61] Much of his scholarly work is particularly on display in his chapter "On Holy Communion" in *The Story of the Prayer Book*, where he combines analysis of architectural data from the early church with early texts like the *Didache* and Justin Martyr's *Apology*, to understand and articulate the roots of Holy Eucharist.[62]

All this said, even the assumption that "British Museum Religion" must be inherently bad is one worth questioning. Gray, for instance, considered the contemporary state of worship in the church and wonders if perhaps this was just what was needed—not only then but even, perhaps, today:

> We see nowadays *ad hoc* decisions in the sanctuary; sloppy dress (clerical collars and trousers showing outside short albs); much wandering aimlessly about the sanctuary; missalettes clutched in the hand; hurried and untidy signs of the cross, genuflections and bowing; bad, ugly furniture and candles dripping wax all over the floor.[63]

Yet, the question of whether or not the imitations of an historical period is an appropriate principle upon which to craft liturgy is entirely valid. However, as we will see throughout this work, Dearmer was not merely interested in the recreation of a distinct historical

---

58. Cited by Gray, "Percy Dearmer," 73.

59. Gray, "Percy Dearmer," 73.

60. Librarian of Pusey House, editor of the Journal of Theological Studies, and author of Liturgies Eastern and Western along with The English Rite: Being a Synopsis of the Sources and Revisions of the Book of Common Prayer.

61. Cofounder of the Mirfield Community of the Resurrection (an Anglican religious order) and author of numerous fundamental texts in the field of liturgy.

62. Dearmer, *Story of the Prayer Book*, 181–220.

63. Gray, "British Museum Religion," 19.

period in worship. Furthermore, the common practice then and now, where the approach to worship is left to the whims of each individual priest does not seem preferable. As Marion Hatchett often remarked, "The rubrics of the *Book of Common Prayer* exist to protect the laity from the eccentricities of their clergy." Dearmer believed the retrieval of an authentically Anglican approach, based upon a clear understanding of historical practices set within the rubrics of the modern *Book of Common Prayer* could strengthen that protection.

In practice, one of the difficulties Dearmer encountered was that his approach was often confused with the Romanizing tendencies of the Ritualists. The most famous story that demonstrates this reality (and Dearmer's response to it) comes from G. K. Chesterton, as retold by Donald Gray,

> They [Dearmer and Chesterton] were walking one day and Dearmer was clad in cassock and priest's gown (not a Geneva gown) and tippet with a square cap. They were met by a party of youths who called out 'No Popery' or 'To hell with Mr. Pope' or, as Chesterton put it, 'some other sentiments of a larger or more liberal religion.' Dearmer immediately produced a precise item of historical and ecclesiological information. "Are you aware," he said, "that this is the precise costume in which Latimer went to the stake?"[64]

Of course, this confusion is not absent from the church today, when changes in liturgy or ritual are often presupposed to be Roman even if they have their actual basis in English Christianity.

Further, this term is often used as a way of dismissing Dearmer as someone who is not an actual scholar of liturgy. But it should be noted that the strength of his work was not in his academic prowess—though his research, as noted earlier, is rather formidable—rather it was that he saw the academic study of liturgy *from the perspective of an artist*. Pure liturgical scholarship had never been his claim nor his goal. As Trevor Beeson put it, Dearmer "was not primarily a scholar concerned with the fine detail of ancient

---

64. Gray, "British Museum Religion," 9.

liturgical texts; rather he was an artist for whom beauty, as well as truth and goodness, was an integral part of religious experience and an essential ingredient to worship."[65]

Dearmer was very clearly a product of many important streams in Anglicanism at the time. However, he did not merely reflect his era in Christian thinking, he molded it. No other Anglican in this period so effortlessly wove together the streams of fully matured Oxford Movement thinking (particularly using Tractarian ideals to counter the excesses of Ritualism) and Christian Socialism with the worship of the church. A student of history—by his own admission, not a scholar—he brought an immensely critical eye to the worship of his day, identifying ideals in Christian worship that would not only prove to be essential ideals of English liturgy but (as we will see) many of which would find their flowering later in the Liturgical Movement. He did indeed delve deep within the history of British worship, but he did so equipped with the strongest theological and social movements of his day. Like anyone, though, there are aspects of his work which do not stand the test of time. To those we turn next.

---

65. Beeson, "Master of Ceremonies," 98.

2

The Limitations of Dearmer's Work

THE POSSIBILITY FOR ANACHRONISTIC criticism is a difficult pitfall of historical scholarship. People are the product of the times in which they live, and even if they prove to be leaders who challenge those times in several areas, there will inevitably be others in which the worldview of the period prevails.

Yet, simply to praise Dearmer's contributions to Anglican liturgy and Christianity would be a hagiographic (and somewhat false) endeavor without also acknowledging the limitations of his work. One of the difficulties with Dearmer is that the few scholars that have undergone significant engagement with his work tend to ignore some of his unsettling failings and limitations. It would be easier to engage in this current revisiting of Dearmer and merely to brush over these rough edges, perhaps with a brief acknowledgement. But a sustained reading of Dearmer's work reveals limitations that come up time and again—limitations that must be acknowledged before worthwhile ideals can be held up as models for contemporary Anglican worship.

The limitations this chapter will engage are based in three different areas. Some areas of his work will not be engaged extensively because of the scope of this particular book. Some limitations of his work are historical and cultural, reflecting views and perspectives with which we would disagree today, but which were common in times past. Some of his limitations as well are strange quirks of liturgical practice or preference that are not clearly tied to his stated ideals. Of course, odd quirks and preferences can be found in any liturgical scholar—indeed, in any person, lay or ordained—who is given charge over the liturgy of the church. An acknowledgment of some of Dearmer's will be helpful in separating some of his preferences from his deeper ideals.

These limitations will thus be traced out in this chapter. Each limitation will be briefly explored, including those places where they seem to reveal a contradiction—or at least a tension—in his own views. Exploring these limitations will ensure this "revisiting" of Dearmer is honest, but also will enable us in the next chapter to focus on the ideals which form the overall thrust of his work and impact upon the Anglican expression of Christianity.

LIMITATIONS OF SCOPE

One of the most significant limitations in a critical analysis of Dearmer's ministry is the scope of the work that can be done. Over the course of his life he wrote or edited over sixty different texts. Though he is best known in modern times for his engagement with liturgy, this was not the only subject upon which he wrote. Indeed, throughout his various books, pamphlets, and tracts, he engaged in a range and variety of subjects, demonstrating his expansive interests and passions.

It is likely that Dearmer's greatest contribution to the life and worship of the church—even greater than the writing he did in the area of liturgy—is the work he did as general editor of *The English Hymnal*, published in 1906.[1] He began his work in Anglican hymnody while at St. Mary's, Primrose Hill. As the use of hymnody grew in Anglican practice, the limitations of *Hymns Ancient and Modern* became increasingly apparent, particularly in areas of poetry and musicality.[2] Dearmer set to work translating ancient liturgical

---

1. Dearmer, *English Hymnal*, 1906.
2. This was not only true in England, but throughout Anglican churches.

The Limitations of Dearmer's Work

texts and casting them in a poetry that was more beautiful. He was joined by Laurence Housman and Robert Bridges. It was then that securing the rising composer, Ralph Vaughan Williams (himself the son of the former Rector of Down Ampney, Gloucestershire), enabled the evolving hymnbook to enrich the heights of musical quality as well. Many of the hymns were first tried out at St. Mary's and the leadership of Dearmer and Vaughan Williams made *The English Hymnal* one of the most significant publications in Anglican church music.

This resulting hymnal, together with the publication of *Songs of Praise* two decades later (in which Dearmer was also significantly involved), forever changed the nature of hymnody in the Anglican tradition.[3] Some of the most famous hymns in the book are *Sine Nomine*, the new tune Vaughan Williams wrote for the hymn "For all the Saints," and "Ye Watchers and Ye Holy Ones," a new text that the Anglo-Catholic Athelstan Riley wrote for the tune *Lasst uns erfreuen*. The hymnal reintroduced plainsong by including several melodies in that tradition in both modernized notation and traditional plainsong notation. Though the use of plainsong was banned for a time by the Archbishop of Canterbury, its use in this new hymnal "undermined the uniformity of the Church of England and successfully challenged the hegemony of *Hymns Ancient and Modern*."[4] The use of *The English Hymnal* eventually spread to churches beyond the Church of England—even beyond Anglicanism itself—and several of its hymns are now beloved by English-speaking Christians around the world.

Another area of significant interest for Dearmer was that of architecture.[5] He wrote excellent books on the history of two cathedrals in the Church of England, describing their architecture

---

As Gray notes, "In a series of lectures in then Philadelphia in 1919, he encouraged his hearers to burn the then current American Hymnal as being deficient in poetry, depraved in sentimentality, and mawkish and provincial in its music." Gray, *Percy Dearmer*, 61.

3. Gray, "Percy Dearmer," 76. For a more in-depth exploration of this work and its resulting editions, see Luff, *Strengthen for Service*.

4. Wilkinson, "History of Hymns Ancient and Modern," 52.

5. One can see this particularly in his small book, *Christianity and Art*.

25

and the pieces of art contained therein.[6] He wrote an extensive guidebook—nearly four hundred pages—for Normandy, filled with architectural notes.[7] He brought much of his research from *The Parson's Handbook* to bear in a 224-page volume exploring medieval altars from the perspective both of architecture and decoration.[8]

His views on architecture will be engaged in this work, but only from the standpoint of how they affect his views on the liturgy of the church. Thus, for example, the specific instructions for altars in *The Parson's Handbook* will not be examined, but Dearmer's insistence that this was a holy place and having this holy place marked as essential will be underscored.[9] If his work is read carefully on questions such as these, it is clear that though he is seeking to articulate the English tradition with such things, he does not do so in order to insist upon their use in all parish churches.

So, for example, though he affirms the rich traditions of curtains about the altar (described in his books as riddel posts with riddel curtains and a dorsal curtain)—a very real tradition in the early church, evidenced in the many instances of ciboria (canopies over the altar which, in ancient times, had curtains hung from the rods between the columns)[10]—his approach to liturgy is not to require that churches reinstate these ancient forms. Indeed, he is quite clear that this model he loves to describe (and which, unfortunately, his work on liturgy is often boiled down to) should not be understood as essential. He writes, "Riddel-posts are not of course necessary, beautiful as they are—and even riddels can be dispensed

---

6. Dearmer, *Cathedral Church of Wells*, especially engaging the architecture on pages 20–86 and *Cathedral Church of Oxford*, especially engaging the architecture on pages 27–56.

7. Dearmer, *Highways and Byways in Normandy*. For example, his analysis of the architecture and stained glass of the church of Grand-Andely (pages 35–41) is stunningly erudite, while remarkably easy to read. Furthermore, his easy tone and quick wit are on display throughout. The book begins with the fantastic phrase, "Everyone knows Normandy, and therefore Normandy is hardly known at all."

8. Dearmer, *Fifty Pictures of Gothic Altars*.

9. Dearmer, *Parson's Handbook* (12th ed.), 75–77.

10. Dearmer, *Church at Prayer and the World Outside*, 107–9.

The Limitations of Dearmer's Work

with."[11] Many read his books and did rearrange their altars according to these ancient traditions, but these forms are not at the heart of what Dearmer believed was essential when it came to the ideals of Christian worship. Along the same lines, the significant time he spends on liturgical colors and vestments[12] will not be engaged in this context, other than to note his insistence that the work of the church requires that we offer our very best.

Finally, Dearmer also wrote extensively on Christian theology. He very much wanted to find ways to articulate Christian truth for the average person. This is most readily on display in a five-volume series he published called *Lessons on the Way: For the Use of Enquirers and Teachers*. Each volume contains thirty lessons that may be used over the course of a church year to offer an introduction to the basic shape of Christian teaching and discipline.[13] He also sought to increase the knowledge of the laity when it came to the worship of the church[14] and its history.[15] He believed that if the average person were able to learn more about the teachings of the church in a simple and straightforward manner, they would be drawn deeper within Christian community.

HISTORICAL AND CULTURAL LIMITATIONS

Other limitations to Dearmer's work when seeking to discern principles for application in contemporary liturgy are found in his historical and cultural context. The laws governing worship in England, particularly in his time, are very different than they are here in the Episcopal Church. Thus, for example, he spends extensive time in the footnotes of *The Parson's Handbook* exploring English

---

11. Dearmer, *Some English Altars*, 3.

12. See, for example, Dearmer, *Linen Ornaments of the Church*.

13. Dearmer, *Lessons on the Way*. The titles of the volumes are Volume 1: *The Christian Covenant*; Volume 2: *Belief in God and in Jesus Christ*; Volume 3: *The Resurrection, the Spirit, and the Church*; Volume 4: *The Two Duties of a Christian*; and Volume 5: *The Lord's Prayer and the Sacraments*.

14. See, for example, *Eight Preparations for Communion* and *The Sanctuary: A Book for Communicants*.

15. See, for example, Dearmer, *Everyman's History of the English Church*.

canon law with regard to vestments,[16] lights upon the altar,[17] and the postures of sitting, standing, or kneeling in worship.[18] However, it is his views on gender and other religions that feel a bit strident to the modern ear.

Some of what Dearmer writes with regard to gender is simply the historical reality of his time. Thus, when confirmation happens, he suggests the genders should sit on separate sides, with a rope between them. He even offers advice on the proper veils that girls should wear.[19] However, beyond those simple items, there are other sections of his work where his language can seem offensive to modern ears. This is made all the stranger because it actually highlights an inner contradiction in his approach, as ideas which seem misogynistic are set beside his strongly held beliefs which encouraged an expanded role for women in the church.

Dearmer's arguments sometimes move to the point of what appears to be misogyny or perhaps even homophobia. He often cites something being "effeminate" as a reason to reject it and goes so far, at one point, as saying, "The present decadence of church ornaments is mainly due to the nuns"[20]—a comment which is baffling because it is offered without explanation, simply a claim that this is "what every Frenchman knows." Elsewhere, he cautions against "anything suggestive of effeminacy."[21] Even in his otherwise sound rejection of lace as a more European than English tradition, he cannot seem to help but include the claim that "ecclesiastical vestments are for men, and it will be a bad day for us if we forget that fact."[22] He clearly believes that women who work at the preparation of the altar are to be blamed for (what he believes is) the poor taste in vestments and altar hangings. All of this sounds remarkably inappropriate to the modern reader.

16. Dearmer, *Parson's Handbook* (12th ed.), 130–66.
17. Dearmer, *Parson's Handbook* (12th ed.), 218.
18. Dearmer, *Parson's Handbook* (12th ed.), 221.
19. Dearmer, *Short Handbook of Public Worship*, 56–58.
20. Dearmer, *Ornaments of the Ministers*, 50.
21. Dearmer, *Parson's Handbook* (12th ed.), 84.
22. Dearmer, *Parson's Handbook* (12th ed.), 129.

The Limitations of Dearmer's Work

And yet, this cannot be pure misogyny because at the same time Dearmer elsewhere encourages the use of both laymen and laywomen in preaching, writing, "For the amount of power that we throw away every year by not using the preaching abilities of women is incalculable. That alone is sufficient to account for half our weakness."[23] When reflecting upon the fruits of the Society of Friends, he praises the fact that their approach to Christianity enabled them to "allow women a place by the side of men in their worship."[24] In his own life, he strongly supported Maud Royden, a former parishioner at St. Mary's, Primrose Hill, who had a calling to ordination that could not be fulfilled in the Church of England. She began preaching at City Temple (a Congregational church in London), causing quite a stir in Anglicanism. Dearmer came to her support, helping to arrange for a "Fellowship Service" at which she would be the minister and he would serve as her assistant, calling it "The Guildhouse." The whole thing was remarkably successful at drawing large crowds. Dearmer left the work after four years to pursue other interests, but the crowds remained strong enough that it continued until 1936.[25] He also notes the limitation of the symbolism in the creeds, being clear that the patriarchal language of the creeds does not properly signify the Holy Trinity, writing, "But words are inadequate: the most perfect phrase can only be a symbol that suggests the truth—even the Fatherhood of God is but a metaphor of one side of parenthood."[26]

Further, when it comes to other nations and religions, Dearmer's views and opinions appear narrow and even slightly prejudiced to the modern reader. Though he does indeed speak of a Christianity that is beyond culture and nation, and though he affirms the importance of a liturgical approach which is authentic to its location, he cannot seem to avoid negative views on other religions and even other Christian traditions. When he devotes a chapter in one book to an exploration of liturgy in the context of mission work, several

---

23. Dearmer, *Art of Public Worship*, 136.
24. Dearmer, "Outward Signs and Inward Light," 176.
25. Beeson, "Master of Ceremonies," 109–10.
26. Dearmer, *Church at Prayer*, 212.

phrases and opinions come off as dismissive of Indian culture and traditional Indian religions.[27]

This uncomfortable dismissal of other traditions is seen most strongly in chapter 4 of *The Church at Prayer*. In particular, his views on the rosary and votive candles are an uncharitable (and not at all accurate) description of these practices in Western Christianity.[28] Also, the rituals of prayer found in Islam (which he also connects, as a negative example, to certain monastic uses of the Divine service), he refers to as "prayer drills" and, with an air of ethnocentric (if not racist) superiority, he declares,

> The psychological effect of this prayer-drill upon men in a certain stage of civilization is profound, and it is notably free from the element of magic; but it has proved powerless to develop men higher than the standard of the average half-civilised warrior, and it does not satisfy a more educated humanity.[29]

As he continues in the third section of this chapter, it also becomes clear that his views on icons (which he refers to as "iconolatry") are not only dismissive, but are joined with those of Keble who likewise rejected the Second Council of Constantinople and its decisions on icons. He does not simply acknowledge they find their roots in a tradition foreign to Anglicanism, but he fully rejects their use while also praising the Western style of religious art (particularly from the Renaissance onward) as being very worthwhile for Christians.[30] The only clear difference seems to be one of a sense of cultural superiority.

Indeed, in some areas of his writing, the cultural superiority with which he wrote descends into blatant racism. One particular section of *Body and Soul* is perhaps the most troubling with regard to race that Dearmer ever wrote:

> The white man has still many faults; but he has moved, while other races have stood still: even the cleverest nations of the East can only advance by learning from him,

27. Dearmer, *Art of Public Worship*, 118–32.
28. Dearmer, *Church at Prayer*, 97–98.
29. Dearmer, *Church at Prayer*, 98–99.
30. Dearmer, *Church at Prayer*, 100–102, and also 116–19.

The Limitations of Dearmer's Work

> for with all its spirituality their religion has been a thing apart... Thus the white man, the product of Christianity, has made his way upward—with many falls and failures, of course—and is today bringing the whole world into conformity with himself.[31]

To be fair to Dearmer, earlier in the chapter it is clear that he is arguing from an assumption (clearly mistaken) that white culture has been entirely formed by Christianity, albeit imperfectly so, in ways that others have not been. Yet, he held a strong belief that the English people alone in the world, following World War I, are most ready to apply Christian principles to international affairs.[32] This was not an uncommon view in the early twentieth century, but it is one that does not stand the test of time.

Similar to his views on women, however, there is not a consistency in his approach. The uncomfortable racism in the earlier section wherein he praised the white race is then followed by a section where he praises examples of Christianity being the force behind the emancipation of woman and the destruction of slavery.[33] Further, he strongly believed that careful attention should be placed in the struggles of the British Empire of his time. He had strong concerns about how Britain was engaging with the various races with which it had interactions.

> When the history of the world is told, it may well be that the real purpose and significance of our national existence will be found to have lain in our behavior to other races, depending for a while upon us, and especially to that wonderful collection of peoples, and races, and tongues which we call the Indian empire. God is the God of all nations.[34]

So, the question becomes whether his uncomfortable and seemingly racist sections—language, it should be noted, that is relatively rare in his writing—are simply a result of the historical and cultural period in which he wrote, or if it was actually evidence of a deeper flaw.

31. Dearmer, *Body and Soul*, 13.
32. Dearmer, *Church at Prayer*, 147.
33. Dearmer, *Body and Soul*, 13–14.
34. Dearmer, *Patriotism and Fellowship*, 101.

Percy Dearmer Revisited

Very early in *The Parson's Handbook*, he praises the preface of the *Book of Common Prayer* with regard to other nations and cultures: "While we claim our right to an English use, 'we condemn no other nations,' a remark which shows how far the spirit of the Prayer Book is removed from the censorious intolerance that once abounded on both sides."[35] He argues strongly that Christianity is not limited to the English or even Western culture and people: "The religion of Christ, if indeed it be the truth, must be too great for any one era, nation, or church to present in its fullness."[36]

It becomes clear as one works through Dearmer's thought that his attempts to draw together an English use were not based upon a rejection of other Christian traditions. Indeed, ecumenism was an important part of his ministry. "We know that there are many Christians without Sacraments who are better than we; and if to deny this is to be untrue, to shirk the question is also to be unfaithful to the truth. We must face it; and only by facing it can we be really loyal to the sacramental position itself."[37] He affirmed the catholic idea that the totality of truth requires attention to the whole and we should resist attempts to say that our beliefs are the best: "Men are generally right when they affirm, and wrong when they deny. By seeking to understand the positive truth which underlies the convictions of other men, we become partakers in the great reconciliation."[38]

What is needed, perhaps, is a sense of proportion. And it is precisely Dearmer's sense of the proportion of things which is often lost on the casual reader or, more commonly, those who have not actually read his work but still find it easy to criticize. Dearmer surely takes some of the blame, not only for the limitations noted above, but also for his propensity to state his views with that endearing or aggravating (depending on your view) tone of superiority and confidence that he is correct. But throughout his work, not only in *The Parson's Handbook* but elsewhere, the sense of proportion remains.

---

35. Dearmer, *Parson's Handbook* (12th ed.), 15.
36. Dearmer, *Church at Prayer*, 6.
37. Dearmer, "Outward Signs and Inward Light," 166.
38. Dearmer, *Body and Soul*, 11–12.

The Limitations of Dearmer's Work

> We habitually judge the religion and character of others by their ecclesiastical politics, by their views upon disputed points, by their neglect or observance of fasts and festivals, of new moons and Sabbaths, or even by the cut of their clothes or the trim of their hair. We are strangely tolerant of hideous and crying evils, strangely acquiescent in selfishness and quiet brutality, so long as our little notions are respected, strangely careless of gross heresies about the very nature of God, because our ears are strained to lesser things. It is not that the lesser things are unessential—they are as essential as fine mouldings are to architecture, as semitones are to music. It is only that we forget their proportions.[39]

Indeed, for Dearmer, the ultimate reunion of Christianity was a definite goal for which the church should strive. And he insisted that this reunion could only happen in a faithful and persistent manner if it were based upon a freedom of view bound up in Christian charity. He insisted that our unity is found in Christ, but that the process of union will take long and arduous work. Further, it would not be found in rejecting one's tradition, but by holding to it critically and with humility.

> Meanwhile the duty of every Christian is clear—to be loyal to every good thing he finds in his own church, averse from every bad thing, indifferent to every indifferent thing; and entirely courteous, modest, sympathetic, and charitable to the members of all other churches.[40]

The whole goal of the Christian life, according to Dearmer, is to move nearer to God. Christianity fails to fulfill its fullest potential when the various traditions settle simply for the increase of their own group. Dearmer truly believed and insisted that when we move nearer to God, we also inevitably move nearer to the truth and nearer to one another.[41]

---

39. Dearmer, *False Gods*, 208–9.
40. Dearmer, *Patriotism and Fellowship*, 56.
41. Dearmer, *Patriotism and Fellowship*, 54–57.

OTHER LITURGICAL QUIRKS

In addition to the limitations noted above, Dearmer also has some liturgical quirks, strongly held views that seem rather strange to the modern reader. Some of these are certainly due to his historical and cultural context, but it is also simply the case that any lay or ordained Christian who has a role in the leadership of Christian worship tends to adapt preferences and ideas that may seem a bit odd to others.

Throughout Dearmer's work, he has a resistance to the use of creeds in worship. In addition to the earlier mentioned worry about the tendency of symbolism to narrow our perception of the divine, he simply does not believe creedal recitations are conducive to the purpose of public worship. He explains his view on this most fully in *The Church at Prayer*, writing,

> First we must face an intellectual method which has become a barrier for many—the practice which has grown up since the tenth century of making the creeds part of normal public worship . . . The recitation of creeds is not an essential part of public worship, as it is not a Catholic practice; and the ancient creeds are not today formulas which everyone accepts. Therefore they are an obstacle, and not a help.[42]

One must admit that this very well might not be a liturgical quirk—it seems slightly out of step with the general thrust of his worship, a rejection of medieval practice based upon a preference for more primitive approaches to worship. In fact, his views here fall into line with a minority view in the current Episcopal Church, which would like to see the recitation of creeds eliminated in our regular Sunday worship,[43] or at least supplemented by other broader statements of belief.[44] It seems unlikely that Dearmer would encourage a public

---

42. Dearmer, *Church at Prayer*, 209.

43. This view has been argued most strongly by one of the founding rectors of St. Gregory of Nyssa Episcopal Church in San Francisco, Richard Fabian, who, in a letter to his bishop, "uses such terms as 'innovative,' 'superfluous,' 'sectarian,' 'retrograde,' and 'non-ecumenical.'" Newman, "To Creed or Not To Creed," 10.

44. See, for example, the approach used in the New Zealand Prayer Book, wherein different affirmations of faith are used depending on the liturgy.

The Limitations of Dearmer's Work

recitation of a newly created creed either. Rather, it is the use of any form of a creed which strikes him as an aberration in the worship of the church.

Other strange liturgical preferences would include his hatred of stained glass, something he believed was not only gaudy and often poorly done but a distraction to the worshiping space of the congregation.[45] He loved the idea of parish bands, a practice which had fallen out of use in Dearmer's time as the use of choirs in the chancel became the custom.[46] He also believed that processions should be reordered, with the clergy properly leading and the people following, a view that has found a new advocate in the work of Neil Alexander.[47] While these various views are interesting, they do not form the heart of Dearmer's work and approach, and thus will not figure prominently in this study.

Certainly, Dearmer is not a person above his time, without failings or limitations in his view and approach. He also had certain liturgical quirks that seem to exist somewhere outside his general approach—though not always outside where some have argued liturgical scholarship should go, even in our own time. But when Dearmer is understood within the context in which he wrote, many of his limitations can be set aside in order to focus on the core thrust of his work. Admittedly, the full corpus of his work was broad and deep enough that the man cannot be revisited in his entirety—at least not in what follows. But having acknowledged the limitations of a full revisiting of the work of Percy Dearmer, our attention may now turn to those ideals of his work which not only stand the test of time but which are worthy of reclamation today.

Anglican Church in Aotearoa, New Zealand, *New Zealand Prayer Book*. Also, the popular confirmation curriculum "Confirm not Conform," which was owned by the Church Publishing from 2009 to 20012, has throughout its iterations maintained a focus on each confirmation class writing their own creed.

45. See, for example, Dearmer, *Parson's Handbook*, 5–6.
46. Gray, "Percy Dearmer," 73.
47. Alexander, *Celebrating Liturgical Time*, 135–39.

3

An Anglican Approach, Neither Catholic Nor Protestant

THOUGH THE MORE STRIDENT controversies of the middle of the nineteenth century had begun to subside by Dearmer's time, there was still a sharp divide between "Ritualist" clergy who sought to cultivate a more Roman approach to worship and "Low Church" clergy who insisted upon the protestant heritage of the Reformation of the Church of England and the *Book of Common Prayer*. Dearmer believed both were mistaken. Indeed, that they had only resulted in creating sectarian parties, he believed, was evidence of the failures of their approaches. Rather, Dearmer first insisted upon renewed attention to the history and sources of the worship of the Church of England, and then for an approach that would not be Catholic or Protestant but instead would be thoroughly Anglican.

ATTENTION TO THE SOURCES OF OUR ANGLICAN RITES

While it might seem that Dearmer's interest was solely in medieval English practices, his starting point for his work was an attempt to ground an Anglican approach to liturgy in the ancient sources of those rites—in particular, the Gallican heritage of our worship. The Gallican rites arose in the fifth century, focused in southern Gaul (modern-day France—there is some evidence that it was used in northern Gaul as well, but the primary place of its usage seems to have been in central and southern Gaul). However, over the years it spread throughout Western Europe and there is evidence of Gallican rites being used in sixth-century Kent, as Queen Bertha likely brought it with her from Burgundy.[1] It was the Gallican rites that wound up serving as the basis for what developed into Celtic liturgical practices.[2]

The Gallican style was more florid, with longer prayers than the ones found in Roman rites. It had greater diversity, with different Eucharistic prayers for seemingly every day within the year.[3] The Gallican rite included many more individual prayers, said in secret by the priest at turning points of the liturgy (for example, while vesting, at the approach to the altar, at the offertory, etc.). Many of these prayers eventually made their way into the Roman liturgy as well.[4] The Gallican rite also had more connections with Eastern elements of liturgy, using more prayers and texts from the East than was common in Roman use.[5] It seems that the Gallican structure of the anaphora (or offering up) of the Eucharistic liturgy was similar to the Antiochene or West Syrian structure.[6] Some argued, as Dearmer noted, that the Gallican and Eastern rites (Dix would add the Mozarabic rite to this grouping)[7] find their similarity in the shared united early liturgy of the church and that the Roman Rite was an exception to that practice.[8] The idea of a shared united

---

1. Dix, *Shape of the Liturgy*, 562–3.
2. Bradshaw and Johnson, *Eucharistic Liturgies*, 193.
3. Dix, *Shape of the Liturgy*, 582.
4. Bradshaw and Johnson, *Eucharistic Liturgies*, 221.
5. Dix, *Shape of the Liturgy*, 549.
6. Bradshaw and Johnson, *Eucharistic Liturgies*, 76.
7. Dix, *Shape of the Liturgy*, 560.
8. Dearmer, *Story of the Prayer Book*, 206.

earlier liturgy has since been discredited by liturgical scholars,[9] but the connections between the varied earlier rites of the church—connections that were originally distinct from what became Roman practice—remain key.

Another way in which the Gallican rites influenced early British practice is found in a curiosity of liturgical archeology. Around twenty lead tanks have been found in Britain, having a liturgical use that cannot be definitely confirmed. They are "wholly unknown on the continent, a category unique to Britain, still puzzling to historians."[10] However, some scholars argue that the fonts were used for the purpose of *pedilavium*, the ceremonial washing of the feet that occurred alongside of baptism, particularly in the Gallican tradition.[11] This seems possible given the practice of adding the *pedivalium* to baptism as laid out in the eighth-century Stowe Missal from the Celtic tradition.[12]

The shift of Christian practice and tradition in the British Isles reached a turning point around 600 CE. Just before the turn of the century, Pope Gregory the Great sent the prior of a monastic community, Augustine, to Christianize the British Isles beginning with King Aethelbert of Kent in southern England.[13] Though Augustine of Canterbury came from Rome, Dearmer noted he was ordained in France according to the Gallican rites. Furthermore, when he arrived in the Isles, it was the remnants of a Gallican rite that was present in Celtic Christianity of that time.[14]

Augustine worked to bring Roman uniformity to the practices of Christianity on the British Isles, work that took several hundred years and several church councils to complete—a strange reality, given the rites of the area of the church from which he came.

9. See, e.g., Bradshaw and Johnson, *Eucharistic Liturgies*, 20–21, 141–53.

10. Lambert, *Christians and Pagans*, 26.

11. So Watts, *Christians and Pagans in Roman Britain*, 171–73, cited by Lambert, *Christians and Pagans*, 28. See a description of this practice in Johnson, *Rites of Christian Initiation*, 170–72.

12. Warner, *Stowe Missal: Volume II*, 24–39.

13. For more information on the background of this mission and the political situation of King Aethelbert, see Lambert, *Christians and Pagans*, 164–71.

14. Dearmer, *Story of the Prayer Book*, 206.

However, Dearmer notes that remnants of the Gallican rites remained even after England formally adopted the Roman Rite. This is seen, for instance, in the Great Entrance of the gifts, a peculiar feature both of the Sarum Use and also of Eastern Eucharistic liturgies.[15] The presentation of a lighted candle to the infant after baptism is another example of an English liturgical custom that comes from its Gallican roots.[16] Dearmer also finds a shared tradition in vesture, noting the Roman criticism of Pope Celestine regarding the Gallican adoption of the pallium by bishops—even though this was only a century before it became common throughout Christianity. However, the pallium was also in common use liturgically at this time in the East, with it even being described as a symbol of the authority of the bishops at this time.[17] What eventually happened during these times was a sort of cross-fertilization, with Gallican rites influencing even practice at Rome.

All this to say, Dearmer believed (and contemporary liturgical scholarship would agree) that the liturgies of Christians on the British Isles developed for centuries independent of Roman influence and, even after Roman influence was enforced, there were continuing debates and controversies over various liturgical practices. These early Gallican and Celtic sources, Dearmer believed, offered a way of understanding an authentically Anglican approach to worship that did not simply borrow from Rome under a mistaken assumption that Rome's practices were more ancient. Further, these ancient sources indicated a strong connection with Christian liturgical practices in the East, a connection that is essential to an understanding of the nature and background of Anglican worship.

NEITHER ROMAN NOR PROTESTANT (NOR EVEN SARUM!)

It is a lamentable fact of Anglican liturgy that Dearmer's work has been assumed to be focused simply on the recovery of Sarum

---

15. Dearmer, *Story of the Prayer Book*, 212.
16. Dearmer, *Story of the Prayer Book*, 234.
17. Dearmer, *Ornaments of the Ministers*, 26–27.

practices as a way of being Catholic and yet Anglican. In actuality, Dearmer found much to criticize in all the parties of the church.[18] More important to Dearmer than one's churchmanship was a well-ordered liturgy that made good use of art and beauty. Dearmer believed that it was poorly done liturgy which had led to the divisive parties in the church: "Neither disorder nor the neglect of aesthetic are normal things. They came into the Anglican Churches through definite historical causes, and produced three parties, Low, Moderate, and High."[19] Thus, he set about trying to craft an approach to worship that could be authentically Anglican and broadly shared.

The first point Dearmer sought to avoid was a simple imitation of the practices of the Roman Catholic Church. The Romanizing wing of the Oxford Movement began in earnest in the early 1840s, led by several followers of John Henry Newman and focused primarily on questions of theology and ethics. Whereas earlier leaders of the Oxford Movement like Pusey had focused on the importance of antiquity in the interpretation of doctrine and discipline, followers of Newman like William George Ward believed the modern Roman Catholic church was indeed "the ultimate repository of doctrinal truth."[20]

In the area of liturgy, earlier High Churchmen had sought to maintain conformity to the rubrics. Even the ritual controversies of the 1840s began primarily with attempts by two High Church bishops, Charles Blomfield and Henry Phillpotts, to enforce rubrics which had become obsolete in practice, ones that had also been insisted upon by Laudians in the early seventeenth century. However, this all remained with an emphasis and claim to conformity to the *Book of Common Prayer*—though many disagreed with the changes.[21]

The early Ritualists of the 1860s began their changes by using the Ornaments Rubric as a clause that could cover a multitude of changes in practice, including the restoration of Eucharistic

---

18. Dearmer, *Parson's Handbook* (12th ed.), 3.
19. Dearmer, *Parson's Handbook* (12th ed.), 2.
20. Nockles, *Oxford Movement in Context*, 143.
21. Nockles, *Oxford Movement in Context*, 214–15.

vestments and vested altars with candles upon them. Thus, a good amount of Dearmer's time is spent exploring the true intention of the rubric. This is an opening rubric, placed directly before the beginning of Morning Prayer in the 1559 *Book of Common Prayer*, which stated,

> And here is to be noted that the minister at the time of the communion, and at all other times in his ministration, shall use such ornaments in the church as were in use by authority of Parliament in the second year of the reign of King Edward the Sixth according to the Act of Parliament set in the beginning of this book.

No small amount of ink has been spent in arguing whether this rubric means the more medieval ornaments common before the changes that happened later in the reign of King Edward should be restored or if, in actuality, it was insisting upon a more minimalist view of ornaments from the 1549 *Book of Common Prayer*.

A significant portion of Dearmer's work was engaged in understanding and arguing for a particular interpretation of this rubric. Indeed, the subject covers nearly twenty pages of the introduction to *The Parson's Handbook*.[22] Though some might believe that the elimination of this rubric would solve all the fuss and controversy regarding the ornaments in worship, Dearmer disagreed. He noted, "In America there is no Ornaments Rubric, but the difficulties are there none the less, and ceremonial vagaries is an acuter form."[23] Further, Dearmer argued that since it was retained in the 1662 *Book of Common Prayer*, it remains an important rubric for Church of England clerics. He argues, rightly so, that it is the only direction given in the prayer book with regard to what the priest is to wear when conducting services.[24] Further, he insists, "The Ornaments Rubric is in fact the 'interpretation clause of the Prayer Book.' It covers all the rubrics which are to follow. Through it alone can they be obeyed."[25] For all these reasons, it is important to acknowledge

22. Dearmer, *Parson's Handbook* (12th ed.), 16-37.
23. Dearmer, *Art of Public Worship*, 113-14.
24. Dearmer, *Parson's Handbook* (12th ed.), 16.
25. Dearmer, *Parson's Handbook* (12th ed.), 17.

some of Dearmer's own views on this rubric. Though the rubric itself is less applicable to today's Episcopal Church, a brief examination of Dearmer's work with the question will be helpful in understanding positions he took throughout his life when it came to the question of vestments and the ornaments of the church.

On a historical note, Dearmer argues that though the interpretation of this rubric is clear to the Anglicans of his time, the reason it was not followed in many churches was because of the liturgical tolerance of the Church of England. He notes that,

> The Puritans were merely non-conforming churchmen, who continued to communicate at their parish churches, and were almost as much opposed to the idea of schism as the high churchmen themselves. Therefore every effort had to be made to allow them latitude until the fury should be overpast.[26]

Thus, the bishops were selective in their enforcement of (what Dearmer believed was) the full meaning of the rubric, hoping to keep the Puritans fully within the bounds of the Church of England. As Dearmer argues, "The bishops found their hands full with trying to enforce the use of the surplice alone, at a time when a large number of clergy insisted on ministering in a cloak, sleeveless jacket, or a horseman's coat."[27]

At the Savoy Conference in 1661, following the Restoration of Charles II, there was an attempt to reconcile the divergent streams within the Church of England. There the Puritans formally objected to the rubric, desiring "that it may be wholly left out."[28] The bishops rejected this and Dearmer notes that they even retained it on its own page, by itself, something later printers changed from the original edition. He argues that they retained the rubric in the hope that, though the Commonwealth had destroyed many of the ornaments of the church, the slightly less reformed practice intended by the Ornaments Rubric was that which would have been found in 1548 (the second year of Edward's reign, according to

---

26. Dearmer, *Parson's Handbook* (12th ed.), 17–18.
27. Dearmer, *Parson's Handbook* (12th ed.), 20.
28. Dearmer, *Parson's Handbook* (12th ed.), 23.

Dearmer's argument,[29] and before the changes of even the 1549 prayer book would have taken place). Following this rubric would result in ornaments that would at least be acceptable to those more conservative and protestant streams in the Church of England. And, Dearmer believed, this was a specific act of restoration, given that the Edwardian prayer book which eliminated many of these ornaments was not in use until the third year of Edward's reign. Further, he argues, "That the Rubric ordered the ornaments of that Book, including the chasuble, was frankly admitted even in the eighteenth century, when the use of the chasuble would have been unthinkable."[30] It was not a rubric well followed, but Dearmer believed that the intent of the rubric was clear when one looked at it historically.

However, unlike some Ritualists, Dearmer did not argue for a militant line on this question. He insisted that when the older ornaments are to be used, it should be with tolerance, moderation, and a loyalty to the use of the Church of England and not the practices of Rome. Further, he insisted that this use should indeed be based upon an examination of the whole Church of England and not even, as some had argued, upon the curiosities of the use at Salisbury Cathedral. What was needed was a faithful approach to ornaments based upon actual English practice.[31]

As the work of the Ritualists grew, their interpretation of the rubric broadened. For Richard Littledale, every aspect of the Roman Catholic Missal which had not been abolished by Henry VIII or Edward VI remained lawful unless there was a specific

---

29. Dearmer, *Parson's Handbook* (12th ed.), 24–32. His specific argument for the dating is found on page 27, where he writes, "The second year of Edward VI was, beyond any doubt, from Jan. 28, 1548 to Jan. 27, 1549. The First Prayer Book received the authority of Parliament in the last week of that year, Jan. 21, 1549, but the Act itself fixes the day on which it is to come into use as the Whitsunday following, June 9, 1549, or if it might be had sooner, then three weeks after a copy had been procured. So that the First Prayer Book could not possibly have been anywhere in use until some weeks (at the very earliest) after the *third* year of Edward VI had begun."

30. Dearmer, *Parson's Handbook* (12th ed.), 25.

31. Dearmer, *Parson's Handbook* (12th ed.), 36–37.

statement in the prayer book forbidding its use—silence permitted all things, he believed.[32]

Older High Churchmen rejected this interpretation. They believed the changes of the Ritualist clergy were just as bad a violation of the rubrics of the prayer book as the excesses of the Evangelical movement. They had sought a renewal of conformity to the rubrics, one that they believed had even garnered acceptance among those in the Low Church party. The older High Churchmen believed that progress had been made in restoring unity to the worship of the church and that now the Ritualists were destroying that very uniformity, using the Ornaments Rubric as a way to upend the ideals of the worship of the prayer book. As Nockles notes, "Ritualism represented the logical outcome of the sectarian tendency in Tractarianism to pursue that which was deemed catholic even at the expense of submission to episcopal authority."[33]

Dearmer's argument with regard to this rubric became less important as *The Parson's Handbook* went through further revisions. As he himself noted in the twelfth edition, the proposed (but failed) *Book of Common Prayer* of 1928 had added a new rubric, "For the avoidance of all controversy and doubtfulness, it is hereby prescribed that, notwithstanding anything that is elsewhere enjoined in any Rubric or Canon, the Priest in celebrating the Holy Communion shall wear either a surplice with stole or with scarf and hood, or a white alb plain with vestment or cope." Dearmer continued, observing, "There can be few reasonable men who will not accept this as the end of a demoralizing controversy."[34]

It was in the second half of the nineteenth century that a division began in the Ritualist Movement. Some believed that, given their claim to be a part of the Catholic Church, "they could not fail to be influenced by developments within Roman Catholicism and to feel themselves to be in competition with Roman Catholics when it came to ritual innovations."[35] Others, however, sought to

---

32. Dearmer, *Parson's Handbook* (12th ed.), 216.
33. Dearmer, *Parson's Handbook* (12th ed.), 217.
34. Dearmer, *Parson's Handbook* (12th ed.), 31–32.
35. Yates, *Anglican Ritualism in Victorian Britain*, 66.

An Anglican Approach, Neither Catholic Nor Protestant

find a way of affirming the catholic heritage and basis of Anglican worship without looking to Rome for a model. Dearmer came from this second stream and eventually became a leading voice for a different approach to Anglican worship: a middle way that was neither Roman nor Protestant (that is, based wholly in the Reformation), but that was thoroughly Anglican and drew its principles from even before Reformation times.

Many of the other ideals of *The Parson's Handbook* are founded upon the clause in the preface to the *Book of Common Prayer* which is clear that national churches have the authority to order their worship in ways that are appropriate to their context and needs. Dearmer insisted that this was entirely in keeping with the precedents of the Catholic Church throughout history—despite, one would assume, the movements toward Roman uniformity throughout the middle ages. He continued, "She has furthermore declared her strong adherence to the best of antiquity; and therefore distinctively Roman practices, which are mainly of seventeenth, eighteenth, or nineteenth-century growth, are doubly opposed to the standard which she sets up."[36] That is, the ancient practices of the Church of England—certainly those present in the early sixteenth century—should provide the resource from which Anglican worship is developed. When Anglicans draw from Roman practices that have developed on their own after the Reformation, they are importing ideas and customs that have no roots in Anglicanism.

Thus, Dearmer argued that specific Roman practices that had become bound up with ideas of what high church liturgy needed to be should be rejected. For example, "The idea that an altar is incomplete (or 'Protestant') without a cross needs to be strenuously combated."[37] In other areas, he rejected Roman importations not only as inauthentic to Anglicanism but also, ironically enough, inauthentic to good Roman liturgy: "Such things as lace albes and fiddle-back chasubles cannot in fact be classed as Roman but simply as a decadent form of art."[38] Throughout his work, he sought to reject

---

36. Dearmer, *Parson's Handbook* (12th ed.), 33.
37. Dearmer, *Parson's Handbook* (12th ed.), 86.
38. Dearmer, *Ornaments of the Ministers*, 48. Dearmer underscores this point by quoting a lecture that Monseigneur Batiffol gave (in Dearmer's words,

45

areas where Roman liturgical choices were being used in Anglican liturgy, often with those who imported them not understanding the history and theology behind the practice they used.

Dearmer also strongly believed that a focus upon the Anglican liturgical heritage would lift up the particular gifts Anglican understandings of worship brought to the wider church. The Offertory as a fundamental aspect of the liturgy is key to this question. The movement of the focus of the liturgy to the consecrating power of the words of administration was, in Dearmer's view, something that shifted the axis of the liturgy entirely.[39] Dearmer's approach to the Offertory is an excellent example of how attentive liturgical choices can manifest profound theological truth—and, Dearmer believed, it was fundamental to the actual work of Thomas Cranmer himself.

> "What Cranmer did," says Professor Burkitt, "and what is still done in the English Church, is to interlace the consecration and oblation of the Sacrament with the communion of clergy and people. In all other Liturgies they are separate." This is a change of the greatest value . . . "[Cranmer] did not go in the direction of Geneva, but in that of St. Augustine. The sacrifice in the Eucharist was to be retained, not done away with as contemporary Protestants demanded, but it was to be the sacrifice of Christians offering themselves."[40]

When the Offertory became a focal point in the liturgy, as suggested by the *Book of Common Prayer*, the Anglican (and Eastern) emphasis upon the gifts of the people being transformed into sacraments of God's grace would then be key to the worship experience.

And yet, to say that Dearmer rejected a Romanizing approach to English liturgy is not to say that he believed in a purely Protestant approach. He clearly came from the stream of the Ritualist Movement that sought to restore ancient liturgical practices to the worship of the Church of England. He would regularly point out the

---

"quite daringly") at an Ecclesiastical Art Exhibition in France, wherein he pleads for a return to more ancient forms of vestments in the Roman church.

39. Dearmer, *Church at Prayer*, 122-23.
40. Dearmer, *Story of the Prayer Book*, 72-73.

An Anglican Approach, Neither Catholic Nor Protestant

failures in understanding that were present in Protestant objections to high church practices. Take the use of the chasuble, for example,

> Even as a church vestment the chasuble was not restricted to bishops and priests. We find it ordered for them in Spain by the Council of Toledo in 633; yet at Rome in the eighth century, the directions for service called *Ordo Romanus I* give the paenula for the acolytes (clerks) and subdeacons also, and the bishop had the pallium as his distinguishing mark; in *Ordo V*, the paenula is mentioned not only for priests but also for acolytes, and the lower orders of the ministry; in *Ordo VIII*, while priests, subdeacons, and acolytes wear it, the deacons take it off and appear in their dalmatics. Nay more—at the present day on the Continent, as we have said, the chasuble is not restricted to priests; for deacons and subdeacons wear it in penitential seasons; and so they did in England until the First Prayer Book restricted the chasuble to bishops and priests. Thus, when Puritans called the chasuble a "Romish and sacerdotal vestment" (words, by the way, which the earlier Puritans used to apply to the surplice—indeed to the scarf and black gown as well), their language was ill-directed: as a matter of fact, it is a peculiarity of the reformed Anglican Church to confine the chasuble to the celebrating bishop or priest.[41]

Not only does the target of Low Church clergy seem to shift as decades come and go (first the surplice is rejected and then, in Dearmer's time, it was affirmed by Protestants as proper to Anglican worship), but they seem often not to understand the history and practice of the very items to which they object.

It is often assumed that Dearmer's response to this controversy was to base his use upon that of the medieval cathedral at Salisbury—that is, the Sarum Use. However, Dearmer explicitly rejected this approach, noting that "the rules of this particular cathedral were altered by the generations that came between their enactment and the second year of Edward VI, and also by the rubrics of our

---

41. Dearmer, *Ornaments of the Ministers*, 46–47.

Prayer Book."[42] Furthermore, by seeking to imitate the Sarum Use, Dearmer believed, attention was not paid to the rubrics and ideals of the *Book of Common Prayer*:

> A great deal of harm has been done by the thoughtless use of the word "Sarum," when the statement of the Prayer Book should have led us to say "English" or "Anglican." This is especially the case in the matter of colours, which are dealt with in a section of this Handbook. It is not to the Rome or Paris of the nineteenth century, nor is it to the Salisbury of the fourteenth, that the Ornaments Rubric refers us, but to the England of 1548. And if some priests break the Rubric in favour of Rome they must not be surprised if others break it in favour of Geneva.[43]

What was needed in the church was attention to the rubric and the history of the Church of England, not imitation of the rites of any cathedral or area.

That is not to say that the resources from the cathedral at Salisbury are not helpful. From the perspective of history, the rising importance of the worship practices in Salisbury began eight hundred years earlier. After the cathedral was moved in the eleventh century to the Bishop of Ramsury's manor on the hill of Sarisberie, a place that eventually became known in Latin as Sarum,[44] the close proximity between the Cathedral and the royal palace at Clarendon resulted in a close relationship between the twelfth-century bishop Roger and King Henry I. When the king was away at Normandy, it was Roger who managed the affairs of the kingdom, laying a foundation for Sarum primacy in all things, whether legal, financial, ecclesiastical, or liturgical. In the thirteenth century, Bishop Richard

---

42. Dearmer, *Parson's Handbook* (12th ed.), 33.
43. Dearmer, *Parson's Handbook* (12th ed.), 34.
44. "The town of Sarisburgh or Sarisberie was thus Latinised as Sarisberiense, but it was usual for scribes to shorten long words, for obvious reasons, and put a line over the shortened area. The line eventually developed into an apostrophe, thus, in such as the Magna Carta, William Longspee is referred to as the Count of Sar' (short for Sarisberiense). This short name was commonly used until, to give it a more credible sound, the common Latin town ending of "um" was added, making it Sar'um." Baxter, *Sarum Use*, 19.

Poore secured royal approval to move and rebuild the cathedral. He chose to move away from the fortified hill to a nearby meadow, thereby establishing New Sarum, later known as Salisbury, the location of the still existing Salisbury Cathedral and the source of the Sarum Missal.[45]

It was Bishop Poore who went to work reestablishing definite guidelines for the life and worship of the Cathedral originally laid down by Osmund, the first Sarum bishop to articulate a definite use. Several documents for Sarum existed over the centuries, some surviving to this day (the one developed by Jocelin) and some lost to history (the one developed by Osmund). However, it was Poore who is usually credited as the originator of the term "Sarum Use." Throughout the thirteenth century and in the following centuries, other dioceses and cathedrals increasingly looked to the documents of the Sarum Cathedral for their own practices. When a cathedral adopted the Sarum Use, much of it would wind up being used in the parish churches of the diocese. When cathedrals were monastic, the parish churches would often follow the Sarum Use as more appropriate than the Benedictine rule of a monastic cathedral. Colleges began to adopt it as well.[46] These rites would have been those in use throughout much of England just before the Reformation and would have been the primary sources upon which Thomas Cranmer based his own revisions in the first *Book of Common Prayer*.

Thus, for Dearmer, the resources at Salisbury had import when trying to understand the history and shape of Anglican liturgy, particularly the intentions behind the rubrics. However, he was also clear that "it must never be forgotten that all the ceremonies of a magnificent cathedral cannot be applicable to a parish church; and indeed we know that they were never so applied."[47] Simple imitation, for Dearmer, will never suffice.

---

45. Baxter, *Sarum Use*, 16–26, 33–35.
46. Baxter, *Sarum Use*, 42–47.
47. Dearmer, *Parson's Handbook* (12th ed.), 33–34.

AUTHENTICALLY AND BEAUTIFULLY ANGLICAN

Instead of simple imitation, Dearmer sought to encourage attention to history and beauty. He insisted, "This is not a question between Catholicism and Protestantism: it is rather a question between pure Christianity and certain comparatively modern developments of it."[48] And, he argued, inattention to history and beauty was just as common in Roman and Continental practice as it was in the England of his own day. "Artists have quite as much quarrel with the church in Latin countries as here: the conviction that Christianity is the enemy of joy and beauty is general abroad, and is justified by the bad art and the morbid delight in suffering."[49] As long as churches were inattentive to beauty and resistant to joy, Dearmer believed, they would continue to drive away those who loved and studied art and who affirmed the goodness in life.

> If they are ignorant of art or acquiesce in its prevalent misuse by the Churches (their sham-Gothic, for instance, their stained glass and shoddy ornament, the bleakness of some, the fussy ceremonialism of others, and the hymnbooks still of most), they must be prepared for the writers, poets, and other artists of all sorts, to be aloof from organized religion, and must not be surprised if these are sometimes hostile to it.[50]

Thus, a true revival in liturgy, such as would actually invite the people of God into the worship of God, would require a new focus and approach.

Attention to history, however, required an authenticity as well—a drawing from the actual practices of a place and not merely the imitation of ideas. Dearmer regularly criticized the "sham Gothic" approach, believing it was emblematic of "the mistaken antiquarianism which dogged the romantic movement in literature."[51] The Patristic or Medieval forms were not, on their own, better

---

48. Dearmer, *Art and Religion*, 45.
49. Dearmer, *Art and Religion*, 45.
50. Dearmer, *Art and Religion*, 89.
51. Dearmer, *Parson's Handbook* (12th ed.), 8.

simply because they were older. The Medieval Latin canon of the mass that would have been used in England had its own problems, Dearmer believed. It was "too long, and unbroken—for it was not relieved by responses and choruses as Eastern liturgies are."[52] No matter the ancient pedigree of an approach, it was still worthwhile to ask critical questions about its authenticity for today's context and whether it resulted in a truly beautiful offering that befitted the worship of God.

So how should ornaments, vestments, candles, and other aspects of the catholic heritage of Anglican worship be used? With tolerance, moderation, and loyalty.[53] Dearmer believed it was only right to affirm that, though in some places more elaborate worship would be appropriate, in other places a simpler approach would be best. Both approaches are needed in the church.[54] In some places, a simpler ceremonial would be fitting, or simpler music: "In many parishes, for instance, a simple form of sung Eucharist is needed after Mattins—a service in which the music is restricted perhaps to a few easy hymns, the ornaments to the plainest vestments, and the ceremonial to the necessary actions."[55]

The goal is not to find one perfect way and to make it uniform. Dearmer believed this was one of the great errors of the Roman approach to worship, the constant drive throughout the centuries to create greater uniformity in worship. Rather, as Dearmer notes, "Uniformity is uncatholic."[56] That some would take Dearmer's work and make parts of his approach to ceremonial essential for all to follow is quite contrary to his own beliefs.

> An idea has grown up in recent years which has done not a little harm: it is the notion that there is one proper and correct way of performing each of the services of the church, and that if everything is not carried out according to some imagined standard, a great offence is done

52. Dearmer, *Story of the Prayer Book*, 72.
53. Dearmer, *Parson's Handbook* (12th ed.), 32–33.
54. Dearmer, *Parson's Handbook* (12th ed.), 31.
55. Dearmer, *Parson's Handbook* (12th ed.), 7.
56. Dearmer, *Church at Prayer*, 164.

> against what is supposed to be Catholic order. It is, of course, true that in each church the duty of the clergy is to obey the rubrics of that church and to follow its lawful customs, and it is equally true that when they prefer their private judgment, they do so to the great detriment of the services . . . but the preceding chapters of this little book will have at least made it clear that there is no one and only way of performing any rite of the church.[57]

True catholicity is that which paid attention to the whole (*kath' holos*, according to the whole, the Greek phrase from which the word "catholic" is derived), not by making the whole look exactly like one part.

Further, when attention was paid to the whole history of the of England, without attempt to demonize any one approach or group, it becomes clear that there is goodness in the attempts of the various parties that have made Anglicanism what it is today:

> We in this little history may well condemn the evil done by a small gang of robbers in the reign of Edward VI, the narrowness of Puritanism, the arrogance and bitterness of both sides; but Puritanism destroyed for us ancient and deep-rooted evils, which helped us to win that freedom today which is the main hope of Christendom—the freedom to go back behind the traditions of men to the plain words and pure example of our Lord Jesus Christ.[58]

If the high and low parties of the church could enter into greater and more fruitful conversation with each other, a truly united and common prayer, expressed in a variety of ways, could finally be found in the of England. While some might think this is only rhetoric, Dearmer believed this was already happening in his own time, as "the so-called High and Low parties of the Victorian era are coming together again, each giving up some of its defects, and

---

57. Dearmer, *Story of the Prayer Book*, 237–38.
58. Dearmer, *Story of the Prayer Book*, 85–86.

An Anglican Approach, Neither Catholic Nor Protestant

both merging in the ideal of an evangelical worship carried out with liturgical beauty."[59]

The use of vestments becomes an instructive example with regard to this hope. As Dearmer noted, "In the Victorian era, when the vestiarian controversy reached its height, ornaments were often used as if their special purpose was to make the clergy hate one another."[60] Thus, those in the more Catholic wing would multiply lace and shorten their surplices into cottas in order to set themselves off from the Evangelicals while the Evangelicals (ironically enough, given prior rejection of the surplice) began to maintain the more ancient and Anglican custom in wearing their surplices long and full. However, they did so not because it was the ancient custom but as a badge and mark which differentiated them from the Catholics! This simply would not do. "We shall never exorcise the demon of party rancor while it is symbolized and perpetuated in externals: but it is in our power today to be more reasonable and more Christian."[61]

At the same time, that is not to say that Dearmer believed we should simply find a lowest common denominator in our worship. Rather, what is needed is charity towards others and breadth of practice within the church. Thus, following the quote above, Dearmer continued by commending the rubric in the deposited (though never authorized) English BCP of 1928 which allowed for the use of choir dress (surplice and stole) or chasuble/cope.[62]

The deposited book of 1928 was, in many ways, a realization of the aspirations of the liberal Catholic wing of the church. Dearmer had been a part of one of the first committees to work on the revision process in England.[63] This is actually one of the places where his connection to Gore in the area of liturgy is most clearly seen. Gore served as president of the Alcuin Club, a group "founded with the object of promoting the study of the History and

59. Dearmer, *Story of the Prayer Book*, 152.
60. Dearmer, *Handbook of Public Worship*, 85.
61. Dearmer, *Handbook of Public Worship*, 85.
62. Dearmer, *Handbook of Public Worship*, 86.
63. Spinks, "Prayer Book 'Crisis' in England," 240.

use of the Book of Common Prayer." Dearmer was one of the fifteen members of the committee, serving as well as the club's secretary and treasurer.[64] The Alcuin Club's proposals, of which both Gore and Dearmer were a part, represented the views of more moderate Anglo-Catholics. When the final version of the 1928 book failed to be authorized, Dearmer was deeply disappointed.[65]

Dearmer's hope was that, after the failure of the deposited prayer book of 1928, a future revision could occur that would lack some of the polemics of that failed attempt. He hoped that revision, occurring after the controversies of the nineteenth and early twentieth centuries, could be truly reflective of the beauty of the Anglican heritage and based upon sound liturgical scholarship. He hoped that it would be an inclusive approach that could draw together the various parties and streams in the of England, "not fearing freedom because there is freedom in Nonconformity, nor beauty because there is beauty in the rest of Christendom."[66] His hope was that the church could finally move past the polemics of the prior age and become "simple in her teaching as the Gospels are simple, and pure in heart as they are pure."[67]

This was not just a matter of good liturgy and taste, but Dearmer believed it was essential to the world in which he lived. Better education and training for clergy, who actually knew the history and ideals of the worship of the *Book of Common Prayer*, were essential to avoid a future in which "the great mass of moderate men will continue to think that the safe and moderate thing is to combine the mistakes of both sides."[68] Dearmer believed that the current situation with regard to Anglican liturgy was only making a mockery of our tradition.

> As it is, the Anglican is still regarded all over the Continent, from Vigo to Vladivostok, as a mere variety of Lutheranism; while a small section of her clergy are

---

64. *Memorial Services*, page i of the back matter.
65. Spinks, "Prayer Book 'Crisis' in England," 241.
66. Dearmer, *Story of the Prayer Book*, 131.
67. Dearmer, *Story of the Prayer Book*, 132.
68. Dearmer, *Art of Public Worship*, 115.

hated by the general public of America and Britain as imitators of Rome, and win the amused contempt of Roman Catholics for their pains. Yet what the Continent of Europe wants, what the whole world is blindly groping for, is what we can offer, what we have always stood for— a reasonable, free, and evangelical Catholicism.[69]

To find that reasonable, free, and evangelical catholicism was the great goal of Dearmer's life and work. He believed it would not come by creating a new "English Use" party (despite the fact that many who read him did precisely that). Rather, a reasonable, free, and evangelical catholicism could only be found when Christians from a variety of perspectives choose to live in deeper fellowship with one another, bound together by their prayer book and shared heritage, and seeking to learn from and be helped by those with whom they disagreed. Dearmer noted that if this was accomplished, then "We each find that those who seem most to differ from us have often the most to teach us, and that often the very men whom we had been taught to oppose have the highest claims upon our admiration."[70] This was the goal, the endpoint, to which Dearmer hoped his work would lead the church.

---

69. Dearmer, *Art of Public Worship*, 115–16.
70. Dearmer, *Patriotism and Fellowship*, 37–38.

4

The Ideals of English Liturgy

DEARMER IS BEST KNOWN among clergy for *The Parson's Handbook*, first published in 1899. Over the course of Dearmer's life it went through twelve editions, in many of them Dearmer responding to critiques of his work and approach, adapting and changing as he sought to create the best possible approach he could.

At the same time, his work and ministry were more than that one book. As one anonymous author noted in a modernist journal following his death, "Many years ago, the writer of this notice on first meeting Dearmer said to him: 'I feel I know you quite well because I know your *Parson's Handbook*.' Dearmer replied: '*The Parson's Handbook* is a very poor introduction to me.'"[1] In his second wife Nan's own writing, she spoke of Dearmer's "disappointment, and later extreme frustration, at a church, and its clergy, who could only focus on the external and ritual aspects of his work and witness."[2] Beyond the *Parson's Handbook*, he was the author of numerous other tracts, articles, and small booklets. The following is an attempt, after an exhaustive reading, to articulate nine fundamental principles to liturgy and worship which guided his works and his approach to Anglican worship, principles that stand the test of time and continue

---

1. Anonymous, "In Memoriam: Percy Dearmer, DD," 115.
2. Gray, *Percy Dearmer*, 60.

FIDELITY TO THE BOOK OF COMMON PRAYER

The most important aim of *The Parson's Handbook*, as identified by Dearmer himself in the introduction to the first edition, was "to help, in however humble a way, towards remedying the lamentable confusion, lawlessness and vulgarity which are conspicuous in the church at the present time."[3] He insisted in that introduction that the confusion and disregard for the rubrics was present among all clergy whether "advanced," "moderate," or "those who dislike all ceremonial." In response, he sought an approach to liturgical practice that paid careful attention to the rubrics of the *Book of Common Prayer* and to the history of practice in the Church of England.

Dearmer's insistence upon the importance of the rubrics for liturgical practice was, of course, founded upon the declaration and vows each priest makes at ordination. However, that is not to say that he believed the rubrics could or even should create a bland, uniform church.

> Freedom to think, freedom to discuss, freedom to develop, are necessary to the very existence of life and truth in a church; but for a priest to omit or radically alter the common services of that church is fatal to the Christian fellowship, and robs the people of their rights.[4]

ND believed that a careful adherence to the prayer book, and to its rubrics, would bring cohesion and unity to the church, but only if her clergy obeyed it.

Furthermore, Dearmer believed that it would push those of various parties to move beyond their own preferences into a deeper question of what the worship of the Church of England should entail. He insisted, "We are to interpret it, not from a Victorian any more than from an Elizabethan, Caroline, or Hanoverian point of

---

3. Dearmer, *Parson's Handbook* (1st ed.), n.p.
4. Dearmer, *Parson's Handbook* (12th ed.), 7.

view, but from that of Scripture, the early church, and the broad Anglican tradition."[5] This broadening was essential for the health and unity of the church.

Dearmer also acknowledged, however, that in times past the question of obedience had been vexed. He clearly found himself on the side of the old High Church clergy who had sought to encourage rubrical conformity despite opposition from the episcopate. "Consequently the 'ritualist' clergy were sometimes forced to disobey the Bishops in order that they might obey the Prayer Book."[6] However, as the Ritualist Movement progressed, it shifted so that even the rubrics of the prayer book were seen to be an obstacle to some people's conception of proper worship. This then created a greater disregard for the rubrics on the other side of the liturgical spectrum as well. As noted earlier, "If some priests break the Rubric in favour of Rome, they must not be surprised if others break it in favour of Geneva."[7]

What was needed now, though, was a renewed obedience to the prayer book of the Church of England. Along those lines, in 1931 the "Worship and Order Group" (of which Dearmer was a member) had a statement at the beginning of his *Short Handbook of Public Worship*, wherein they insisted,

> Religion follows ceremonial practices and the habit of diverting obedience from the Prayer Book—the document which the Lambeth Conference sets up as the standard of doctrinal teaching—to the service books or directories of other churches inevitably leads to the transference of the inner allegiance of heart and mind, in theology as in religion.[8]

The prayer book itself, Dearmer argued, was based upon New Testament teaching and founded upon a Reformation standard of worship that insisted "upon the need of daily Bible reading in

---

5. Dearmer, *Parson's Handbook* (12th ed.), 35.
6. Dearmer, *Parson's Handbook* (12th ed.), 3.
7. Dearmer, *Parson's Handbook* (12th ed.), 34.
8. Dearmer, *Short Handbook of Public Worship*, iv.

the mother tongue at 'the Common Prayers in the Church.'"[9] The Litany of the prayer book, one of its most underused aspects, was the first piece of liturgy translated by Thomas Cranmer, predating even the prayer book itself. Dearmer argued that its use before the Eucharistic liturgy represented the ancient practice of the church.[10] It is not that the prayer book is an entire manual for how worship shall take place at all times and places. "Like its immediate predecessors, the medieval missals, it is meagre in its ceremonial directions, leaving much to ancient custom."[11] But the standards of the prayer book as its own approach to worship—quite different than other contemporary approaches that existed—must be followed for worship to be authentically Anglican.

Furthermore, the argument that the rubrics of the prayer book are impossible to follow as they are written is an argument that Dearmer rejected outright. He believed that this claim was often just an excuse for the imposition of a cleric's own personal views.

> It is often lightly assumed that many of the Prayer Book rubrics are impracticable. When that is indeed the case, permission should be sought from the Ordinary before they are put aside; for the Curate of a church should always be in a position to account for everything that is done within his cure. But as a matter of fact, the impracticability of a rubric generally vanishes when an attempt is made to practise it.[12]

Worship that was faithful to the ideals and rubrics of the prayer book—a real possibility often ignored by clerics—would not only be more faithful and authentic, it would also function in a didactic and evangelistic manner. "If we showed people the Eucharist better, we should need to talk about it much less, which would be a great gain, at home as well as in the mission-field."[13]

---

9. Dearmer, *Story of the Prayer Book*, 3.
10. Dearmer, *Story of the Prayer Book*, 216.
11. Dearmer, *Parson's Handbook* (12th ed.), 36.
12. Dearmer, *Parson's Handbook* (12th ed.), 270.
13. Dearmer, *Art of Public Worship*, 124.

Before concluding this section, a few comments must be made about the practice of extemporaneous worship in the church. One might assume, given Dearmer's insistence upon loyalty and obedience to the prayer book, that he was wholly opposed to any extemporaneous practices of worship. However, he believed that extemporaneous worship had an essential place in the church—and not just from a missionary standpoint. Rather, "It secures the necessary element of freedom; furthermore, it may bring spontaneity and vitality into a service, and is a good corrective to formalism."[14] Dearmer worried about Anglicans who were only able to pray by the book, who had lost the ability to use their own words and prayer and, more importantly, who had lost the ability "for the silent prayer which is above words altogether."[15]

This is not to say that Dearmer believed clerics should allow significant portions of worship be their own extemporaneous offering. The forms of worship in the prayer book should still be the foundation of the church's worship. The great English author, John Milton, was active in church debates during Oliver Cromwell's Commonwealth in the seventeenth century. Milton was strongly opposed to liturgical forms, but Dearmer's response to Milton's views is excellent:

> Milton's mistake was, in fact, a very simple one. He thought that every minister would be a Milton. He did not realize what a deadly thing average custom can be, what a deadly bore an average man can make of himself when compelled to do continually a thing for which he has no natural gift. He did not foresee the insidious danger of unreality and cant. We should all, of course, flock to hear Milton praying extempore, if he were to come to this life again; but there are many mute, inglorious ministers whom we would rather not hear.[16]

Thus, Dearmer affirmed the comprehensive nature of Anglican spirituality, a spirituality that would be incomplete without

---

14. Dearmer, *Story of the Prayer Book*, 8.
15. Dearmer, *Story of the Prayer Book*, 11.
16. Dearmer, *Story of the Prayer Book*, 10.

extemporaneous prayer and times of silent prayer (of which he praised Quakerism as a great example). However, that comprehensiveness still required, at least in the Anglican tradition, maintaining the properly authorized forms of worship.

> There is some loss in the use of printed words; but there is a greater gain. We have in them the accumulated wisdom and beauty of the Christian church, the garnered excellence of many saints. We are by them released from the accidents of time and place. Above all, we are preserved against the worst dangers of selfishness: in the common prayer we join together in a great fellowship that is as wide as the world; and we are guided, not by the limited notions of our own minister, nor by the narrow impulses of our own desires, but by the mighty voice that rises from the general heart of Christendom.[17]

The common prayer of the church functions as an organism which unites and enlivens the body of Christ, not only freeing the people from the frailties and perspectives of their clergy (and themselves) but uniting them with a church that is much larger than our own opinions.

THE IMPORTANCE OF BEAUTY AND ART IN CHRISTIAN WORSHIP

Dearmer's own approach to the *Book of Common Prayer* was one that paid careful attention to art, taste, and beauty. As Nan Dearmer recounts in her biography, his use of artists in the development of the worship space at St. Mary's, Primrose Hill, resulted in warm affections between him and the artistic community. One of them, C. O. Skilbeck, said, "We always told P.D., 'You are the artist's priest. No other cleric understands the artist as you do, and we understand you.'"[18] Thus, this approach came from his own skills and gifts—and, of course, his aforementioned childhood with an artistic father.

---

17. Dearmer, *Story of the Prayer Book*, 11.
18. Cited by Dearmer, *Life of Percy Dearmer*, 123.

The modern difficulty, Dearmer believed, was a popular misunderstanding about the relationship between Christianity and art. He argued that many have long assumed that Christianity existed in opposition to art. At best, people have believed that the church took up art as a tool during the Middle Ages, when the church was already corrupt and filled with superstition. The result of these erroneous views, Dearmer believed, was "the general notion among pious folk in the nineteenth century was that art was rather wrong, while poets and artists of Europe generally considered that religion was rather stupid."[19] Drawing Christianity and art back together, given such interaction between the two in recent centuries, was, Dearmer believed, an even more difficult (and more pressing) task than the reconciliation of science with religion.[20]

The more extreme low church wing of the Church of England had furthered this divide for explicit and theological reasons. As Dearmer believed was so often the case, they took a fair criticism too far:

> The Puritans (like St. Bernard) felt that the vision of God was obscured by decorative display. It is true also that excess of ornament is a real danger, and that beauty itself is lost when the need of simplicity and sincerity are forgotten. But there was also the insanity of a wild reaction, a kind of Romanism turned inside out. Because the Roman Catholic Church (in common with the whole of Christendom up to the sixteenth century) acted on the obvious truth that beauty is a good thing, the growing Puritan party paid Rome the compliment of embracing ugliness for her sake.[21]

Dearmer therefore believed that he had to contend both with Roman excesses (which he often objected to on the grounds of taste) and Puritan refusals. But the work, he believed, was needed and essential to the faithfulness and future of the Christian church.

---

19. Dearmer, *Christianity and Art*, 3.
20. Dearmer, *Parson's Handbook* (12th ed.), 6.
21. Dearmer, *Story of the Prayer Book*, 81.

The Ideals of English Liturgy

At one level, Dearmer emphasized beauty and art as a way of drawing people back to the church. "In his early ministry he constantly pleaded on behalf of those driven away from the church on aesthetic grounds."[22] Indeed much of his opening chapter in *The Art of Public Worship* is devoted to the claim that church attendance had been dropping in his day because the sense of artistry had almost entirely left the services, resulting in long, tedious, and poorly done liturgy to which, Dearmer says, he would be surprised if anyone wanted to go.[23]

However, Dearmer eventually acknowledged that good liturgy would not solve all questions when it came to filling churches. According to Gray, he remained "confident that worship done well, in beautiful surroundings, with good music, can be evangelistic, and therefore it is our solemn duty to take the greatest possible care over everything we do in church."[24] Dearmer himself wrote, "There will be no sudden response, no flocking back into churches that have been chilled so long. Only if we do what is right, for the sake of the right, all will come right in the end."[25] Patience and a commitment to the ideals of beauty and art would be needed for some time before true change could come. It is true, the population never did flock back into the churches . . . yet Dearmer's point remains that the goal should be doing things well. Chasing a program that will produce a dramatic increase in numbers was never his priority.

For Dearmer, beauty and art were not only important and helpful aspects of Christian worship, they were essential. This was the foundation of his approach to liturgy throughout his life, not only a mere question of taste, but one that arose from his theological beliefs. "If you ask me, 'How can art be a necessary part of the worship of God, if its motive is beauty?' I reply, 'Because beauty is the manifestation of the Father; and this is precisely what modern Christianity has forgotten.'"[26] One sees here the developed understanding of the Ritualists looked at from a slightly different angle,

---

22. Gray, "British Museum Religion," 17.
23. See Dearmer, *Art of Public Worship*, esp. 4–9.
24. Gray, "Percy Dearmer," 76.
25. Cited by Gray, *Percy Dearmer*, 143.
26. Dearmer, *Art of Public Worship*, 7.

one that drew from the insights of the incarnational theology of the *Lux Mundi* movement. In Dearmer's view, beauty can become a particular mode of God's revelation. The incarnation of the Son is the fundamental ground of all divine revelation, but Dearmer believed that beauty was also its own manifestation of the divine life. For that reason, beauty and art were not only essential to the church, they were essential to all of life. "The object of art is not to give pleasure as our fathers assumed, but to express the highest spiritual realities. Art is not only delightful; it is necessary."[27] Or, as he said elsewhere, "Art is a necessary of the spiritual life. Civilisation cannot exist in its absence, for without it civilisation is but organized savagery."[28]

Dearmer acknowledged that Christianity—particularly Western Christianity—has not always found ways to express this theological truth well. He believes that though true Christianity should always affirm beauty and art, skepticism about them existed even in the early church.

> From very early times a strain of asceticism, which crept in from pagan religions, has tainted Christian thought. We find it in the second century among the heretical Marcionites, who refused baptism to those who lived in wedlock, and among the Montanists (also heretics), compared with whom our seventeenth-century Puritans were sybarites.[29]

This stream in the church was one that was so strong, that he doubted that a full affirmation of the arts in the life of the church would come about until the church reached a new and different era of existence.[30]

One way the church could begin to grow in its affirmation of the arts, Dearmer believed, was by being attentive to religions that did not have the inherent Western suspicion of all things beautiful. For example, he praised the Zen doctrine of art as found in Buddhism, "The idea that art is a kind of Zen, or digging down to the divine within

27. Dearmer, "Preface," v.
28. Dearmer, *Art and Religion*, 11.
29. Dearmer, *Art and Religion*, 46.
30. Dearmer, *Christianity and Art*, 36.

The Ideals of English Liturgy

us . . . one form of the meditation and mental concentration whereby men obtain access to that part of their nature which is universal and divine."[31] Dearmer believed the sacramental life of the church could help Christians reconnect with this universal truth. "Art, then, has always been what Christianity is—sacramental; for both are true to life and appeal to man in his completeness. The artist has always felt intuitively what Christianity has revealed as a principle."[32] It was sacramental language that would be able to provide the best definition of what art truly is: "Beauty cannot really be defined: it is an ultimate category of thought: but we might define art by saying that art is the expression of spiritual values in terms of beauty."[33]

The correction to this error in the life of the church, though, would not be found solely through better theology of art and the sacraments. Rather, it requires the church to reach out to and affirm the artists in our culture. "If the artist needs us, we need also the help of the artist to set us straight, to restore our balance, to help us in the attainment of the complete image of God."[34] The problem is that the church has often believed she had the artistic skills needed for good liturgy on her own. As Dearmer notes with his characteristic wit, "The bishops have seldom troubled to consult good writers, and have acted as if they thought the art of prose composition was miraculously conferred upon them at their consecration."[35] The leaders of the church must recognize their limitations. In the same way that Christian leaders reach out to skilled professionals in so many other areas of Christian life, they must likewise reach out to the most skilled in art when it comes to the worship of the church.

Dearmer hoped a change in this area could be made, though the inadequate philosophy and theology of the church in this area had fostered a stream that did not affirm beauty and art. That is not to say that beauty comes above doctrine. Rather, it is that true beauty will flow from good doctrine. "It was even forgotten that the true

---

31. Dearmer, *Christianity and Art*, 8.
32. Dearmer, *Body and Soul*, 16.
33. Dearmer, *Art and Religion*, 11–12.
34. Dearmer, *Art and Religion*, 91.
35. Dearmer, *Art of Public Worship*, 46–47.

purpose of outward things is to express inward beauty and truth, that in fact doctrine must, in a healthy church, rule ceremonial."[36] We must, therefore, begin to live into a practice of worship that affirms the teachings of the church, particularly the incarnation. "Given poetry to handle in the text of our common worship and its ceremonial, we have used it all as if it were prose; and this is only another way of saying that we have made material use of spiritual things."[37]

Much of Dearmer's advice, therefore, contained practical ideas that could advance the ideal of art in Christian worship. Once we understand that the goal of Christian worship is "to secure some reflection of God's nature while it expresses man's adoration,"[38] we can make specific choices that will advance that goal. One simply must be willing to set standards high—and to set those standards in consultation with experts and leaders in the fields of art, literature, and in music.

In his own time, Dearmer praised the advances being made in hymnody (advances he was very much a part of), expressing approval that the hymnody of the church "has grown in its charitable comprehensiveness, has steadily improved in words and music, and has won for itself a place deep in the heart of the people."[39] That improvement needed to be continued and expanded throughout the music of the liturgy, led by the priest:

> A parson is not necessarily a musician, but he is responsible for securing certain broad principles which are both musical and moral. In the first place, he must insist on the fact being recognized that normal musical parts of the service are the Psalms and Canticles, Kyries, Creed, *Sanctus*, and *Gloria*, and these, with the hymns, must be sung properly before any time is given to the anthems.[40]

As Dearmer argued over and over again throughout his life, often doing less—but with higher quality—will do much to enhance the

---

36. Dearmer, *Short Handbook of Public Worship*, iv.
37. Dearmer, *Short Handbook of Public Worship*, 89.
38. Dearmer, *Parson's Handbook* (12th ed.), 1.
39. Dearmer, *Story of the Prayer Book*, 127.
40. Dearmer, *Parson's Handbook* (12th ed.), 189.

worship of the church. Thus, he believed that parish choirs should be smaller than they are and also should sing better than they do.[41] Large surpliced choirs could actually, Dearmer believed, be a detriment to the worship of the church when they became a replacement to the musical education of the parishioners.[42]

Along the lines of "less is more," Dearmer believed that churches should focus their financial resources on the purchase of vestments and ornaments that were of the absolute highest quality—referring to workmanship, not merely price. "It is better for poor churches to buy a good thing in simple material than a bad thing in more expensive material."[43] His rejection of the use of cottas is often not due simply to their Roman heritage. Rather, he believes they are often used because they are simply more cheaply made than a fully gathered traditional alb or surplice:

> Now the worship of Mammon has so far intrenched on the honour due to God that the sweater has his own way with us, and it is considered seemly for a minister to appear in church in a garment called a 'sausage-skin,' a so-called surplice that is not only short, but is entirely deprived of gathers, so that a few extra half-pence may be saved from the cost of worship.[44]

To do something well, in good quality, is what is most important. The desire for well-done liturgy and ritual is innate. Dearmer noted that at funerals, "even those who dislike 'ritual' on other occasions are most grateful for its comfort at this time."[45] What is needed is a church that does not merely copy the pomp of the world but that brings theologically thoughtful beauty and art to bear on its worship.

---

41. Dearmer, *Parson's Handbook* (12th ed.), 46–47.
42. Dearmer, *Parson's Handbook* (12th ed.), 46.
43. Dearmer, *Parson's Handbook* (12th ed.), 92.
44. Dearmer, *Parson's Handbook* (12th ed.), 128.
45. Dearmer, *Parson's Handbook* (12th ed.), 426.

Percy Dearmer Revisited

SIMPLICITY IS BETTER THAN ELABORATE CEREMONIAL

In practice throughout *The Parson's Handbook*, Dearmer sought to offer what would be the greatest possible ceremonial practice. He was explicit that this was not because each and every church should follow such elaboration,[46] but because "to do otherwise would leave the more extreme church to 'the too tender mercies of the fancy ritualists.'"[47] Before giving instructions for the celebration of a service of Holy Communion, for example, Dearmer is clear, "The priest's duties are described with special fullness in this chapter, and most of the authorities for the directions given for the other ministers will be found in the foot-notes of Chapter XII. The maximum is necessarily given: but simplicity is best."[48] Furthermore, "The details are not meant to proclaim an elaborate ceremonial as the writer's ideal for the English-speaking people."[49]

Dearmer was aware, however, that there would be people who would take his *Parson's Handbook* and seek to replicate all the small details he offered as possibilities. For this reason, what he enjoyed significantly was when he was given the opportunity to write shorter books that were not focused on offering the full range of options and possibilities. As he wrote in the introduction to his *Short Handbook of Public Worship*, "In a volume of more encyclopaedic character it is almost impossible to avoid the impression that the author's desire is to make ordinary church services elaborate, which has always been opposite to his intention."[50]

His ideal of simplicity was founded upon the prayer book itself. Liturgy in the middle ages had become exceedingly complex and difficult. The baptismal liturgy, for example, "was lengthy, complicated, and repetitious, being a conflation of a long series of rites administered in the late Roman Empire to adult converts, and entirely

---

46. Dearmer, *Parson's Handbook* (12th ed.), 1.
47. Gray, *Percy Dearmer*, 41.
48. Dearmer, *Parson's Handbook* (12th ed.), 306.
49. Dearmer, *Parson's Handbook* (12th ed.), 1.
50. Dearmer, *Short Handbook of Public Worship*, xiv.

in Latin with the exception of an exhortation to the godparents."[51] Cranmer's goal when he revised the baptismal liturgy, therefore, "was to simplify the baptism service and make it accessible to understanding."[52] Another issue of complexity in liturgy before the *Book of Common Prayer* was the Daily Office. As Dearmer notes,

> By the time of the Reformation the legendary element was so bad that "to lie like a second nocturn" became a proverb; and the services—besides being said at inappropriate hours in a language not understood by the people—were in a state of such extraordinary complication that—to repeat our quotation from the preface of the English Prayer Book—"many times there was more business to find out what should be read than to read it when it was found out."[53]

Thus, one of the fundamental goals of the prayer book was a simplification of the various rites and ceremonies of the church, "without detracting either from their grace, significance, or richness."[54] There is great irony, then, that people took Dearmer's ideals of liturgy and simply turned them into another complex task to be done, an approach which undermined Dearmer's understanding of the very goal of the prayer book for worship that is not only in the language of the people but that, in its action and movement, it is also intelligible to the people.

An example of Dearmer's emphasis on simplicity where others would prefer complexity is the question of lights in the worship space. He insisted that the only pieces of liturgical fabric that need to be changed with the season were the frontal and vestments.[55] He rejected oil lamps as smoky and unbecoming to worship. Rather, "All lighting, whether in nave or choir, should be of as simple and unobtrusive a nature as possible."[56] Though he affirmed candles

---

51. Jeanes, "Cranmer and Common Prayer," 34.
52. Jeanes, "Cranmer and Common Prayer," 34.
53. Dearmer, *Story of the Prayer Book*, 161–62.
54. Dearmer, *Parson's Handbook* (12th ed.), 40.
55. Dearmer, *Parson's Handbook* (12th ed.), 60.
56. Dearmer, *Parson's Handbook* (12th ed.), 50.

upon the altar (against those who claimed they were too Roman), he rejected the importation of the Roman style which resulted in a multiplicity of candles. He thoroughly rejects the custom of six "office lights" on the gradine, insisting that only two lights on the altar should be used, that this is the ancient and universal custom until the nineteenth century.[57]

Some churches even today, particularly of a higher liturgical style, keep the custom of the six "office lights," insisting that they are lit for the offices and the two candles upon the altar are only lit for Eucharistic liturgies. However, it might be noted that not only does Dearmer reject this practice but it is contrary to the 1979 *Book of Common Prayer*'s "Order of Worship for Evening." Following the Prayer for Light and before the *Phos hilaron*, that "candles at the Altar are now lighted, as are other candles and lamps as may be convenient."[58] The norm in the 1979 prayer book is for the candles upon the altar to be lit at any public service of worship, be it an Office liturgy or a Eucharistic liturgy. As Dearmer notes, "There is no authority whatever for reserving special candles for use at mass; the same candles were always used for other services; nor are such things as 'vesper lights' known to the church."[59] That is, Dearmer's careful scholarship and arguments on this question wound up affirmed later in the work of the Liturgical Movement.

Much of what passed for Ritualism in Dearmer's time, he believed, was the result of an uninformed accretion of practices. He noted that this "has always been the vice of religious ceremonial, details being added which come to be regarded as of sacred obligation as the generations pass, and in the end destroy the significance and the beauty of the original rite."[60] However, when one instead focused on the actual traditions of the church, as understood in history and enshrined in the prayer book, it becomes clear that these traditions are not extravagant. "They are really restraints

---

57. Dearmer, *Parson's Handbook* (12th ed.), 87.
58. *Book of Common Prayer*, 112.
59. Dearmer, *Parson's Handbook* (12th ed.), 90–91.
60. Dearmer, *Parson's Handbook* (12th ed.), 1.

upon private extravagance."[61] The problem, Dearmer believed, with many Ritualist clergy is that their guide was primarily their own personal views of reverence, whereas the tradition of the church "is essentially moderate and subdued."[62]

Beautiful and faithful worship was also best maintained by attention to one's liturgical space and context. There were far too many churches, he argued, that went for a larger approach to ceremonial and ornaments, resulting in "the crowding of servers in a small space."[63] In many smaller churches, Dearmer encouraged them to avoid trying to fit a surpliced choir in the chancel and instead to have stalls for the clergy and a few seats for the servers.[64] Further, the music itself should be glorifying to God and edifying to the people. Dearmer lamented that "there are many choir-masters who are not even artists enough to prefer a simple service well sung to a pretentious one sung badly."[65]

Rather than an excess of ceremonial action, what was important is a level of care and attention to detail. When mistakes were made, as was bound to happen, Dearmer urged clergy and servers not to whisper to each other but rather to speak quietly and calmly in a natural voice, as this would attract less attention. "A mistake matters little, if no one makes a fuss about it."[66] Whereas Christ rejected formalism in his own religion, an obsession to the minutiae of tithing mint, dill, and cumin, Dearmer noted that he "had no hard word against ceremonial."[67]

Attention to ceremony should not mean an insistence upon uniformity—a tendency Dearmer believed was thoroughly Roman. This, along with the attempts to fit fragments of Roman ceremonial into Anglican liturgies, only resulted in bad worship. "But things

61. Dearmer, *Parson's Handbook* (12th ed.), 39.
62. Dearmer, *Parson's Handbook* (12th ed.).
63. Dearmer, *Parson's Handbook* (12th ed.), 32. Contrary to this tendency, Dearmer quotes Cicero, "Caput artis est decere quod facias." That is, "The chief thing in any art you may practice is that you do only the one for which you are fit."
64. Dearmer, *Parson's Handbook* (12th ed.), 46.
65. Dearmer, *Parson's Handbook* (12th ed.), 190
66. Dearmer, *Parson's Handbook* (12th ed.), 215.
67. Dearmer, *Parson's Handbook* (12th ed.), 11.

done for the sake of convenience and simplicity will be perfectly correct."⁶⁸ Though the directions in ceremony might seem overwhelming at first, that was because far too many clergy and lay leaders had not been taught the simple and natural way to carry out worship. He believed it was the same as manners, which, in everyday life, involved rules that could be seen as rather elaborate. They did not seem elaborate to adults because adults learned those rules from their childhood.⁶⁹

Dearmer also finds simplicity to be key to the development of liturgical vesture. He makes the (hopefully by now well-known point) that clerical vesture is actually merely ancient Roman ordinary clothing. But he also notes that as this vesture became more associated with clergy, yet was still in use in with the secular world, there was an emphasis upon a simpler approach in the style worn in the church over and against what was found in society. Thus, when commenting on the mosaic in the Chapel of St. Venantius in the Lateran baptistery, he writes, "This mosaic, like others in which lay officials appear, brings out clearly the fact that, whereas lay costumes are decorated, the clerical costumes are plain, except for the simple *clavi* on tunic or dalmatic. The clergy in fact wear attire which is simple as well as out of fashion."⁷⁰

Even Dearmer's rejection of silken colored chalice veils (so common in today's churches) is not only based upon their lack of history but also upon the fact that they make things more cumbersome than they should be.

> It will be noticed that *the only veiling* of the vessels by the priest is the veiling with the spread corporal after the communion. There is no Anglican authority for silk chalice veils, which were of late origin and were introduced into this country in the Victorian era. They became popular because they supplied (with coloured stoles) an opportunity of using liturgical colours in churches where coloured vestments were not worn. They are clumsy things to handle; and the priests who have discarded

---

68. Dearmer, *Parson's Handbook* (12th ed.), 296–97.
69. Dearmer, *Parson's Handbook* (12th ed.), 39.
70. Dearmer, *Ornaments of the Ministers*, 31.

The Ideals of English Liturgy

them can testify to the relief which comes when the vessels can be handled without a silk veil which drags at the paten and requires to be arranged and rearranged.[71]

If clergy would focus less on doing liturgy in an impressive manner and more on doing what is simplest and the most natural, the worship of the average congregation would greatly increase not only in quality, but also in its impact upon the people of God.

THE COOPERATIVE WORSHIPING COMMUNITY

For Dearmer, the laity form the basic unit of the church and are the source from which Holy Orders and Christian mission should flow. In his book on the history of the English church, he praises the Italian Marsiglio of Padua, who rejected the increasingly strong claims of the papacy and hierarchy of the church. He praised Marsiglio's arguments as being early stirrings of Reformation thought in the early fourteenth century.

> He pointed out that St. Peter had no authority over the other Apostles; that the appointment of ecclesiastics rests not with the Pope but with the community of the faithful, as is shown by the appointment of the first deacons in Acts vi. 2–6; that the Catholic Faith is one, and rests on Scripture only, but when any doubts arise they are to be settled by a general council of the faithful, in which laity and clergy alike have seats; and that the Roman bishop, though he should act as president of such councils, could have no power of coercion, of interdict, or excommunication beyond what the council might choose to confer. This book of Marsiglio, the first example of modern scientific method, began the Reformation.[72]

In the Anglican tradition, the voice and views of the laity has only increased in focus over the years. Indeed, prior to the revisions to ecclesiastical governance in the Church of England in the late nineteenth and twentieth centuries, the role of the laity through

---

71. Dearmer, *Linen Ornaments of the Church*, 18.
72. Dearmer, *Everyman's History of the English Church*, 69–70.

Parliament had long been one of the principles of established Christianity in England.[73] In 1970, General Synod sought to enshrine that same principle.

Over and over again, Dearmer argued that Ritualist clergy far too often ran over the ideas and views of the people, violating their voice in worship by ignoring the norms of the *Book of Common Prayer* or celebrating liturgy in such a way that the priest becomes the center of attention.

> Clericalism is a constant danger in all forms of religion; but the Anglican Church is essentially not clericalist, and therefore she does not unduly exalt the minister by putting the people at the mercy of his own ideas in prayer, or by enthroning him in a pulpit at the east end of the church to overshadow the congregation. The set forms of prayers, the eastward position, the ministerial vestments, the cooperative service, the appointed gestures are all to hide the man and to exalt the common priesthood of the Christian congregation.[74]

Dearmer urged clergy to be careful about their movements. "He should not poke out his hands in front of him, nor let his eyes wander over the congregation... He must never sidle along the altar nor stand at an undecided angle."[75] While it may be helpful in preaching for one's individual character to come through, this should never be the case when leading worship. "In saying the services the priest's individuality should be as unnoticeable and his actions as normal as possible."[76] Thus, the ancient traditions of the church—once more, put into practice thoughtfully, simply, carefully, and in conversation with history, theology, and art, can overcome the clericalizing tendency in Christianity.

Whenever exploring ideas or changes, Dearmer constantly tested them against what he believed would be edifying to the people of God. This is seen on full display later in his life, when he wrote a

---

73. Stevick, "Canon Law," 225
74. Dearmer, *Parson's Handbook* (12th ed.), 216.
75. Dearmer, *Parson's Handbook* (12th ed.), 215.
76. Dearmer, *Parson's Handbook* (12th ed.), 246.

small book arguing strongly (and with quite a bit of research) that the increasingly popular requirement of fasting communion for all people was not only wrong from an historical and theological point of view, but was wrong because it failed to be attentive to the needs and abilities of the average parishioner.[77]

Even in the regular worship of the church, he held up the importance of the people's participation, insisting that those roles given to laity should be held up and affirmed—but in a way that respected the role itself. Thus, for example, those who read Scripture should be those who can truly read it well.[78] All of this was in strong contrast to the practice of Ritualist clergy who, through the increase in choral masses and non-communicating attendance, often decreased congregational participation. Thus, Dearmer's approach here was much more in keeping with the Tractarians who had advocated higher practices but through approaches like Gregorian chant so that the people might be encouraged fully to participate in the worship of the church.[79]

Dearmer longed for clergy who would focus more on teaching the people of God so that they might take a stronger role in the life of the church. He expressed dismay that the old rubric in the 1662 *Book of Common Prayer* for catechesis to occur during Sunday Evening Prayer had become almost entirely ignored in his time. He urged clergy, when they were able to get attendance at evening services, not to offer a second sermon but to offer basic Christian instruction instead.[80] Even when sermons were offered, he believed they should be more catechetical and less feats of rhetorical skill.

> [The people] are disappointed, because only a few preachers have marked psychic [here, he means the psychological powers of persuasion] powers, and they deserve to be disappointed. The man who can rightly wield to their extreme limits these tremendous unseen weapons in complete purity of heart and with full intellectual power

---

77. Dearmer, *Truth about Fasting*, esp. 2–13.
78. Dearmer, *Short Handbook of Public Worship*, 13.
79. Herring, *Oxford Movement in Practice*, 233.
80. Dearmer, *Parson's Handbook* (12th ed.), 391.

comes, like John Wesley, once in a century; and we must plan our immediate campaign without him.[81]

Just as in extemporaneous prayer, even though some clergy may be able to preach with great rhetorical skill, this does not mean that it should become the standard for Christian preaching in all contexts. It is clear that he affirmed the older Tractarian insistence that education and teaching should be a key focus of preaching and must precede and undergird any changes in liturgical practice.

In architecture, he urged churches to build a comfortable fellowship hall leading into the church, a place where people of all classes could gather and build community. "The people will never really pray in our churches till they are at home in our churches; and a home is a place where folk love one another."[82] He championed a revival of the agape (love feast) of the ancient church, hoping that over time they would move from the fellowship hall into the very church itself,[83] itself a part of the Parish Communion movement.

TRUTH AND AUTHENTICITY IN WORSHIP

Though the practice of some congregations and clergy who value Dearmer comes across as a sort of English preciousness, Dearmer's own view was that liturgy and worship should be true and authentic to the community itself. One of the greatest examples of his frustration with contemporary practices was found on the mission field, where English practices were often put into place even though they made no sense in the missionary culture. The following quote, in which his cultural and racial condescension reflect his historical context, illustrates the issue quite well:

> I used to notice in the tropics that the nice little brown choirboys sweltered in cassocks and horrid little tight surplices. Why was this? Was it because the good missionaries were afraid of their catching cold? No. It was because, long years ago, when the missionaries were at

---

81. Dearmer, *Church at Prayer*, 217.
82. Dearmer, *Patriotism and Fellowship*, 64.
83. Dearmer, *Patriotism and Fellowship*, 64.

> home, they were accustomed to the choirboys wearing cassocks, in order to keep them warm, and still more to hide the fact that the bigger boys had impossible trousers, which looked ridiculous under the horrid little surplices. Now, in the tropics you obviously want nothing of the sort. You just want your choristers in nice albes, or—cooler still—in decently long rochets, with their brown ankles and bare feet appearing underneath.[84]

Notice, he does not advocate doing away with vestments or simply using the clothing that is common to another area and culture. Rather, he argues that aspects of the Anglican tradition can indeed be put into practice in ways that are authentic and appropriate to a different culture. While a modern liturgist might very well find a different solution that Dearmer suggested, the ideal of looking for one that is careful in how Anglican traditions are used is worthwhile.

Another danger of inauthenticity in worship, for Dearmer, was the recitation of the confession on a weekly basis. He quotes a line from the confession in the 1662 *Book of Common Prayer* ("The remembrance of them is grievous unto us; the burden of them is intolerable") and then asks, " Is that generally true in our mouths today? Do most members of a congregation really find the burden of the sins they have committed, since the early service last Sunday, intolerable?"[85] His worry as well was that the regular practice of general confession would keep people from the important work of examination of conscience. Here he quotes John Ruskin, "Nothing in the various inconsistency of human nature is more grotesque than its willingness to be taxed with any quantity of sins in the gross, and its resentment at the insinuation of having committed the smallest parcel of them in detail."[86] This is not to say that he was an advocate for requiring private confession. In fact, he was quite clear that "the Prayer Book does not contemplate routine confession; and the clergy have no moral right to go beyond the principles laid down in the First Exhortation."[87]

84. Dearmer, *Art of Public Worship*, 126.

85. Dearmer, *Art of Public Worship*, 77.

86. Ruskin, *Lord's Prayer and the Church*, 37. Cited by Dearmer, *Art of Public Worship*, 79.

87. Dearmer, *Parson's Handbook* (12th ed.), 63.

Interestingly enough, Dearmer actually resisted the Decalogue in regular worship as well for the same reason—he believed it was inauthentic to our modern understandings of life and ethics. For example, we do not believe in creationism anymore (the command for the Sabbath day in Exodus is based upon the creation narrative). Further, we believe that parental responsibility is just as important as that of children (even though the Decalogue focuses wholly on responsibility to parents).[88] It is not that Dearmer did not agree with the Decalogue. Rather, he feared that a recitation of it might distract more than help because of its increasing distance from the lived experience and knowledge of modern culture. Liturgy that required the people to state facts and beliefs that are not actually held by Christians is not liturgy that is authentic and faithful.

INFORMED USE AND DESIGN OF LITURGICAL SPACE

As noted earlier, Dearmer wrote extensively on the design and decoration of liturgical space. Those that would follow Dearmer, however, by simply setting up an English-style altar and thinking this brings them into the English tradition are sorely mistaken. Rather, what was most important was that the decisions and use of a liturgical space be theologically and historically informed.

Along these lines, it should be noted that although Dearmer does encourage the chancel to be up at least a step from the nave, he does so because it is an aid to the ability of the people to hear the liturgy. It is not, he would argue, to help people see. "A church is not a theatre, and it is not necessary or even advisable that the action in the chancel should be displayed with great prominence."[89] Along these same lines, he did encourage the use of riddel and dorsal curtains around the altar, based upon their connection with the ancient ciboria which set the altar off as a holy space.[90] However, the goal was not simply to imitate a Medieval practice, but was to encourage clergy to think carefully about the more important and

---

88. Dearmer, *Art of Public Worship*, 70–71.
89. Dearmer, *Parson's Handbook* (12th ed.), 46.
90. Dearmer, *Church at Prayer*, 107–9.

The Ideals of English Liturgy

primitive tradition as finding ways to treat the altar as a truly holy object in our worship. Curtains and riddel posts may do it well, but they are not what is essential.[91] What is essential is the design and use of the space conveying a sense of the sacred.

Dearmer did not encourage clergy to ensure altars had crosses upon them and, further, he rejected the arguments of those who believed they were essential.[92] The best position, he believed, for a cross was for it to function as a rood on the chancel screen or, when there is no screen, on a beam running across the chancel arch.[93] He did not care for the use of the stations of the cross either, noting that they are explicitly tied to a liturgy which was not authorized in the Church of England at that time. He also rejected them on the view that they focused too much on Christ's death instead of the rest of his life, work, and resurrection—and that some were based upon tradition and not Scripture.[94]

The font should be properly placed at the entrance of the church and should, he believed, be made of stone if such is possible. He argued that English fonts never were placed in baptismal chapels.[95] Here he is very much correct, given the architectural evidence. Baptism was often reserved to bishops and places of worship would often not be allowed to have their own baptistery. There is seventh-century evidence still existing of "the licensing of an oratory on the express condition that it should have no baptistery."[96] Many supposed early examples of baptisteries were actually chantries which were later turned into baptisteries.[97] He insisted that baptismal fonts should be filled at each baptism, according to the rubrics, and that "the Puritan practice of putting 'pots, pails, or basins' in it to hold the water was steadily condemned by our bishops from Parker downwards."[98]

91. Dearmer, *Some English Altars*, 3.
92. Dearmer, *Parson's Handbook* (12th ed.), 86.
93. Dearmer, *Parson's Handbook* (12th ed.), 50–51.
94. Dearmer, *Parson's Handbook* (12th ed.), 62.
95. Dearmer, *Parson's Handbook* (12th ed.), 60–61.
96. Davies, *Architectural Setting of Baptism*, 56. See also 56–58
97. Davies, *Architectural Setting of Baptism*, 60.
98. Dearmer, *Parson's Handbook* (12th ed.), 61.

Percy Dearmer Revisited

THOUGHTFUL MOVEMENT

Not only the design of liturgical space, but the way in which the people and ministers move within that space is also essential. Dearmer argued that the essence of public worship—from a psychological standpoint—is actually primarily the ceremonial (that is, the action) and not the ritual (that is, the form and language of the rite). He argues that worship can occur without words but it cannot occur without action, because even silent meditative prayer is the cessation of action—a change of action in and of itself, interestingly enough. Worship that has theologically thoughtful movement will be more successful achieving its goal—not the cultivation of religious thoughts but "the orientation of the whole self towards God."[99]

The first movements to be considered are those of the laity. Dearmer commends the seventeenth-century canon which encouraged the people to bow to the altar when they arrive and exit the worship space. He was clear, however, that the tradition of the church is to bow to the altar and not to the cross. He also commends the practice of bowing at the name of Christ and at the Gloria Patri. When it comes to the Holy Sacrament, he strongly advocates for the practice of kneeling to receive (as was required in the rubrics of the 1662 *Book of Common Prayer*). On the question of genuflection (dropping to one knee in reverence before the Holy Sacrament), Dearmer insists that this is not the practice of antiquity nor is it found in the worship books of the Anglican tradition before or after the Reformation. When the Latin *genuflexio* is used in some books (such as the Missal of Hereford), Dearmer argues that it means to kneel.[100]

Dearmer does not, however, affirm the practice of kneeling during the Creed—though he does encourage bowing at the incarnation clause, including the crucifixion. His reasoning, once more, is based not only on his understanding of the Anglican texts but also because for one person to drop to a knee creates a disturbance in worship.[101]

Indeed, the best posture for worship, Dearmer insists, is that of standing. He insists that this was the original attitude for Christian

---

99. Dearmer, *Art of Public Worship*, 81.
100. Dearmer, *Parson's Handbook* (12th ed.), 229–35.
101. Dearmer, *Short Handbook of Public Worship*, 43.

The Ideals of English Liturgy

prayer, as seen in early Christian art which consistently depicts a standing orans position.[102] Further, he notes that it was even the case in cathedrals that often the choir would remain standing with the altar party during the Eucharistic prayer.

The norm of Eucharistic action when it comes to the ministers should be a celebrant with a deacon and subdeacon. Dearmer acknowledges, "Some people imagine that the deacon and subdeacon are a sort of enrichment suitable for a ritualistic church, and that they ought only to be present when an elaborate ceremonial can be carried out. There could hardly be a greater error."[103] He insists that this division between a high mass and a low mass is a Roman innovation. The use of a deacon highlights this order as an order of ministry in the church and the use of a clerk (or, in some contexts, a lay person fulfilling the role that had been given to the subdeacon in pre-Reformation times) highlights the role of the laity in the Eucharistic action.

When the ministers go in procession, Dearmer urges them to remember that a procession has an objective and is a significant act of worship on its own. Whether it is a procession to the Rood, the Lord's Table, or the Font, it should draw people to the liturgical action and object. He insists strongly, "A procession is not the triumphant entry and exit of the choir, nor is any such thing known to the church as a 'recessional.'"[104]

Dearmer encouraged churches to order their space so that the clergy sat facing east, just like the people. Sitting north and south was a modern innovation he did not care for and facing west, he felt, often resulted in the clergy simply staring at the people. Further, when clergy sit facing east, Dearmer suggested, they could help keep unruly choristers under control.[105]

When the time comes for the leadership of prayer, the movement should be simple and restrained. "This parting of the hands should not be done too obtrusively. The arms should never be swung about, nor the hands moved with rapid gestures; but every action should

---

102. Dearmer, *Short Handbook of Public Worship*, 48.
103. Dearmer, *Parson's Handbook* (12th ed.), 284–85.
104. Dearmer, *Parson's Handbook* (12th ed.), 254.
105. Dearmer, *Parson's Handbook* (12th ed.), 48.

be done with simplicity, solemnity, and restraint."[106] He believed that this was actually the best way for the priest to show reverence—not by individual small manual actions throughout the liturgy, but by standing "in the great Eucharistic Prayer with hands outstretched and heart uplifted in the central act of Christian worship."[107]

The offertory should be a significantly highlighted action in the Eucharistic liturgy (as noted earlier). At the same time, Dearmer advised, "it does not look well for the priest to carry out the alms-basin as if it were his own private booty." He also rejected the addition of an offertory to the Evensong liturgy, noting that the offering of money should always be connected to the bread and wine offered in Holy Eucharist.[108] When the bread and wine are brought forward, he argued that the admixture of the water should happen in advance, believing that the preparation of the bread and wine should be a singular act so that when they are brought they are ready to be blessed and used.[109]

Dearmer also argued strongly against the custom of veiling the chalice in advance of the Great Thanksgiving. "For the veiling of the vessels is (by a special rubric in the Prayer Book) a sign that they contain the consecrated elements, and to veil them at the beginning of the service is to destroy the significance of a special act of Eucharistic reverence."[110] This resonates with his earlier advice against even using colored chalice veils.

In the baptismal liturgy, Dearmer argued for the more primitive practice where Communion and Confirmation would immediately follow baptism, arguing that the separation of them is a curiosity of liturgical history.[111] It is worth noting that, once more, here he is very much in keeping with the more ancient practice of English Christianity. There were many controversies surrounding the divergent liturgical practices Augustine of Canterbury

---

106. Dearmer, *Parson's Handbook* (12th ed.), 197.
107. Dearmer, *Short Handbook of Public Worship*, 52.
108. Dearmer, *Parson's Handbook* (12th ed.), 247.
109. Dearmer, *Parson's Handbook* (12th ed.), 278.
110. Dearmer, *Parson's Handbook* (12th ed.), 154.
111. Dearmer, *Story of the Prayer Book*, 221.

encountered in the late sixth century, as he sought to reassert Roman control over the English church. Among those controversies, Lambert notes, "Augustine believed there were flaws in their [the English church's] administration of the rite of baptism."[112] Thus, Bede records Augustine not only challenging the British date of Easter but also urging the British bishops "to complete the Sacrament of Baptism, by which we are reborn to God, according to the rites of the holy Roman, and apostolic church."[113] The Latin here is instructive, "ut ministerium baptizandi quo Deo renascimur iuxta morem sanctae Romanae et apostolicae ecclesiae compleatis."[114] By requiring a "compleatis" or "fulfilling, finishing"[115] of Baptism, he is using language similar to that used to describe what became known as the rite of confirmation. Williams notes that "In the *Life of St. Brigid* we read of a vision where two priests anoint the head of a girl, 'completing the order of Baptism in the usual way' (ordinem baptismi complentes consueto more)."[116]

One of the most likely explanations for Augustine's criticism is that the British Christians were still practicing the older custom of presbyters chrismating baptismal candidates, thereby "confirming" their baptism. The Roman practice by this time, however, restricted this act to the ministry of bishops. When the post-baptismal episcopal anointing first arose, sometime in the fourth-century, it was not without its critics.[117] Jerome believed the practice related "more to the honour of the ministry [of the episcopate] than for the principle of necessity."[118] He allowed for the custom because of its possible connection to the gift of the Spirit and the Apostles, but he still insisted that the baptized candidate may receive the Spirit without the prayers of the bishop. Thus, as Williams notes, "When, therefore, Augustine demanded that the Britons should complete baptism in

112. Lambert, *Christians and Pagans*, 179.
113. Bede, *Ecclesiastical History of the English People*, 106.
114. Bede, *Histoire Ecclésiastique de Peuple Anglais*, 294.
115. Stelten, *Dictionary of Ecclesiastical Latin*, 49
116. Williams, *Gildas: The Ruin of Britain*, 270.
117. Johnson, *Rites of Christian Initiation*, 160–61.
118. James, *Origins of the Roman Rite*, 20.

the same way as the Roman Church, he was asking them to give up this custom."[119] As Bede relates the story, it seems that the British bishops resisted Augustine's authority on this matter, recognizing that the ancient practice of their people with regard to the rites of initiation would indeed be difficult to change. It is worth noting that Dearmer's own view on this question has held up quite well and been affirmed by further liturgical scholarship in the twentieth century.

Dearmer also argued for the practice of baptism by immersion, if possible, noting, "it is a pity that immersion has gone so entirely out of practice; and in warm weather, if the sponsors wish it, the child should be dipped (three times according to the First Prayer Book), but 'discreetly and warily.'"[120] In this area, his advice does not seem to have been heeded by many, but it still remains the recommendation of liturgical scholars today.[121]

In each one of these areas of liturgical movement, Dearmer's concern is not only for historical and ecclesial authenticity, but also for the theological implications of the liturgical action chosen. To think of that which is practical is not enough. Careful consideration must be given to what liturgical actions highlight and show forth concerning the theological truths of any given liturgical rite.

SOCIAL JUSTICE AND THE ETHICAL IMPLICATIONS OF WORSHIP

Many of Dearmer's views on social justice have already been noted. The most significant remains that extreme care must be taken so that vestments and church furnishings are not procured at the expense of fair labor. He was a strong advocate of the Arts and Crafts movement in the Church of England and spoke strongly in the original introduction to the first *Parson's Handbook* "about preachers in sweated [created in sweatshops] surplices and cassocks pointing to a cheap cross upon an evilly produced altar, all unconscious of the

---

119. Williams, *Christianity in Early Britain*, 474.

120. Dearmer, *Parson's Handbook* (12th ed.), 384–85. See also Dearmer, *Story of the Prayer Book*, 222.

121. See the arguments of Turrell, *Celebrating the Rites of Initiation*.

social misery involved in the making of such ornaments."[122] He abhorred what he called "sham-Gothic" churches that he argued were often made out of the wealth of the industrial movement, wealth made at the expense of the poor and working class.[123] Christians must pay heed to where the objects and buildings they use in worship come from, otherwise they run the risk of beginning worship with a poisoned root.

Dearmer also believed that the use of printed services was an aid in bringing together various classes of people when they worshiped. He noted that while some people prefer extemporaneous prayer, both upper-class and working-class people often prefer liturgical forms, "the one because the old prayers are better, the other because they are better known. All classes can combine most easily in a common form of service which is at once simple and profound."[124]

Most importantly, Dearmer taught that the Christian life is not primarily about following a ritual well. He pointed out,

> In this [Jesus] seems to have differed from all his subsequent followers: they have taught that it is wrong not to pray regularly and often; he, on the contrary, taught that it is wrong not to love God and man ... Jesus did not preach prayer as a religious duty, but took it for granted as he found it, and urged that it should be purified by simplicity and love. What he taught and sought in people—and found in the most unlikely of people—was goodness.[125]

Dearmer believed that it was the inability of people to grasp this truth that lay behind the hypocrisy for which the world so often scorns the church: that religious people are often rather unpleasant. He argues, rather forcefully, "A man may pray seven times a day and may spend many hours upon his knees, but if he prays to the wrong god, or if he prays with a bitter heart, his prayer will not

---

122. Dearmer, *Parson's Handbook* (12th ed.), 4.
123. Dearmer, *Short Handbook of Public Worship*, 70–71.
124. Dearmer, *Church at Prayer*, 173.
125. Dearmer, *Church at Prayer*, 41.

make him more religious."[126] Good and faithful liturgy will change the worshiper—but the worshiper has to be willing to be changed.

A DISTINCT SENSE OF HUMOR

The final principle of Dearmer worth noting is his distinct sense of humor. It could be painful, certainly, to be the target of his biting wit. However, it was his easy style of writing and the sense of humor found therein which made him so popular for so many clergy and lay people. A few choice selections from his writings will perhaps illustrate this gift:

> The sides of the pulpit should not be so low down that the hands dangle helplessly: Englishmen as a rule find their hands rather in the way, and they will speak much better, and avoid fingering their garments much more, if they can rest their hands quite comfortably on the sides of the pulpit.[127]

> The congregation will often have cause to be grateful if there is a clock within sight of the preacher.[128]

> The Gospel . . . It is right that the gospeller should be preceded to the chancel step by the epistoler (carrying the book) and the clerk, who will then stand on his right and left, facing him as he reads. When people thought that the north was inhabited by evil spirits, there was perhaps some meaning in the reader turning in that direction; but now that we know it to be inhabited by Scotsmen, the gesture seems uncalled for.[129]

Regarding embroidery on vestments,

> The principle of distinguishing our services by a difference in costume seems to be a sound one; and one

---

126. Dearmer, *Church at Prayer*, 23–24.
127. Dearmer, *Parson's Handbook* (12th ed.), 54.
128. Dearmer, *Parson's Handbook* (12th ed.), 55.
129. Dearmer, *Short Handbook of Public Worship*, 42–43.

The Ideals of English Liturgy

doubts if there would have been much objection to it, if it had not been felt that the clergyman sometimes looked rather like a sofa-cushion.[130]

I remember that one chaplain at a highly important centre of government was so pleased with his Parade Service that he had it printed. He ought to have added a culminating touch to his work by printing these *preces* at the end of the service:—"℣. I have done those things which I ought not to have done. ℟. And I have left undone those things which I ought to have done.[131]

A danger in Christianity, particularly among those who study the practice of liturgy, is always to take matters too seriously. Though Dearmer had no trouble, clearly, articulating strong opinions, his humor somehow made them more palatable. The principle of using humor to address a difficult situation has now become a standard part of good pastoral practice, particularly given the insights of Edwin Friedman, who noted that the use of humor can "keep things loose" when anxiety might begin to run high[132]—as it often does in questions of liturgy and worship.

Each one of these nine principles could in many ways be applied to the best of liturgical thinking even in our own time, regardless of denomination. However, Dearmer held that the theological and historical heritage of the Anglican tradition raised them up as particular to the Anglican tradition's practice of Christianity.

---

130. Dearmer, *Handbook of Public Worship*, 83.
131. Dearmer, *Art of Public Worship*, 135.
132. Friedman, *Failure of Nerve*, 242.

5

Conclusion—Dearmer Revisited

IN SOME WAYS, DEARMER was remarkably ahead of his time, anticipating and advocating some liturgical changes that have now become commonplace, particularly in the Episcopal Church, such as the priority of Eucharist as the principal liturgy on Sundays and the practice of public baptism in the community as opposed to private baptisms with only the family.[1] Dearmer advocated strongly for full communal participation in worship,[2] an approach that has been realized in several ways throughout contemporary Anglican worship.

At the same time, there are valid criticisms to make of his work. As already noted, the assumption that an explication of one particular historical period can provide a framework for contemporary worship has been doubted by many. Of course, the "Ornaments Rubric," upon which his work was founded, is absent from the American prayer book along with the prayer books of several other provinces of the Communion. The question of whether or not the liturgical practices of the time mentioned in the Ornaments Rubric should still dominate is a fair one (though, of course, each group in Anglicanism does seem to want to idealize its own portion

---

1. See Gray, *Percy Dearmer*, 157–59.
2. Dearmer, *Art of Public Worship*, 100.

Conclusion—Dearmer Revisited

of history).[3] This all raises the question that has long dogged Dearmer—is his approach too "English" to be applied to liturgical contexts outside the Church of England?

This question of historical and liturgical methodology is particularly pressing given the ecumenical nature of today's Christian church. The Liturgical Renewal of the mid to late twentieth century saw a great convergence of worship practices among denominations and the fear might be that a returned emphasis upon an "English Use" might also signify a return to a more sectarian age. It is rather clear that even in Dearmer's time, his advocacy of an "English Use" came, at times, from a very strong nationalism and anti-Catholicism that is rightly uncomfortable to many contemporary Christians.[4] At the same time, his ecumenical arguments in other places are stunning. See, for example, this short quotation in a small collection of essays about silence in other Christian traditions,

> Perhaps that is the reason why the separated bodies, starting with so few advantages, have yet brought forth such wonderful fruits of the Spirit. They often had that which is vital, which is central. They lost what was good, but sometimes they won what was better. Some, for instance, lost episcopacy, but won freedom; some lost Sacraments but won the Holy Ghost; some lost priests and won prophets.[5]

One gets a sense throughout his work that he had a strong admiration for Quaker traditions, interesting given his views on liturgy. Dearmer was clearly not a sectarian through and through. Rather, he believed that one could hold on well to one's tradition while still learning from the riches of other traditions.

All this said, I would argue that insights and goals of Dearmer's work do indeed need reasserting today. At times our ecumenical age has seen the importation of practices absolutely foreign to an Anglican liturgical and theological understanding. There are Episcopal congregations adapting practices like "confirmation stoles,"

---

3. See Chapman, *Anglican Theology*, 77–101.
4. See, e.g., Gray, *Percy Dearmer*, 179–81.
5. Dearmer, "Outward Signs and Inward Light," 183.

seeking to jettison the creed from worship, and even contemplating practices like the virtual consecration of Eucharistic elements. Throughout, the idea that seems to have arisen in contemporary liturgical practice that church is primarily about a show people watch. Some of this understanding is because of ecumenical engagement and (at times) a jealous importation of the popular success of modern evangelical worship which is indeed often focused on a well-done show.

Given all of these realities, it is important to look carefully at Dearmer's ideals and see whether they can enable contemporary Anglicans to do worship well, in a way that is faithful to the theological principals of our tradition, edifying to the people, and also attentive to our local contexts. The vast majority of clergy do care deeply about the worship of their congregations and I do believe that Dearmer's ideals can be grounding principals for the average parish priest, rooting us in the best of our Anglican tradition.

First, attention will be given to how Dearmer's ideals influenced his approach to the question of incense and worship. Then, Dearmer's ideals will be put into conversation with contemporary liturgical questions to see how well they hold up in contexts that are not exclusively English.

A TEST CASE: THE JUDICIOUS USE OF INCENSE

The question of the use of incense is perhaps one of the more controversial in Anglicanism—both in Dearmer's time and today. His approach provides a test case in which many of Dearmer's principles are put into practice.

First, care and wisdom is needed on the part of clergy. Incense cannot be outrightly condemned without ignorance to the traditions of Scripture and the church. At the same time, it should not be forced upon a congregation without a sufficient amount of conversation, teaching, and discernment. As Dearmer notes, "To condemn the simpler use of it would be to go contrary to God's Word written, in the New Testament as in the Old; although it would be wrong to introduce its use where the people do not desire it, as it is wrong in

Conclusion—Dearmer Revisited

any other way to interfere violently with tradition."[6] He argues that in the normal parish incense is often an unneeded introduction and that it should only be used when desired by the people.[7] If incense is to be introduced at all, it should be after discussion with the people. Dearmer himself would encourage it to be done through a mechanism like the Church Council in England.

Attention should be paid to the rites and language of the *Book of Common Prayer*. Though the 1662 prayer book of Dearmer's time did not include reference to incense (outside of its reference in psalmody and in Scripture readings), contemporary Episcopalians can note its reference in the 1979 *Book of Common Prayer*. It is mentioned both in an opening sentence and a collect of the Evening Prayer rites, along with a direction for its use (if that is desired) in the Lucenarium and the Consecration of a Church.

Conversation about its use might include whether it adds or distracts from the beauty of the community's worship—a decision that should not be made unilaterally. And if it is used, Dearmer would hold to the importance of simplicity, suggesting it only be used on great festivals and even then with a sense of moderation.[8] He believed the exaggerated use of incense in ritual was actually one of the main reasons people found it so objectionable, writing,

> The elaboration of "censing persons and things" was gradually introduced in the Middle Ages; and in the modern Roman Catholic use which unfortunately was imitated by some English clergy-men, this became tiresome in its excess, the officiant walking about the altar and nearly thirty times clanking fussy little swings. This has not reduced the dislike of incense among our fellow-countrymen; and of the normal parish it is always true that nothing excites stronger feelings than incense, in spite of its scriptural character and widespread use in the Christian church, and that of nothing is the indiscriminate introduction more unwise.[9]

6. Dearmer, *Parson's Handbook* (12th ed.), 11–12.
7. Dearmer, *Parson's Handbook* (12th ed.), 30.
8. Dearmer, *Parson's Handbook* (12th ed.), 225.
9. Dearmer, *Short Handbook of Public Worship*, 32.

Care would need to be taken that the space was thoughtfully considered for what is censed when, that it is done in keeping with the ideals and theology of Anglican worship. Dearmer would also be very concerned to know about the manufacture not only of the thurible, but of the charcoal and incense itself, wanting to be sure it was done in the context of just and fair wages. A cheap thurible made in a factory under unjust conditions, one that burned chemicals and artificially contrived incense, simply would not do.

So, attention should be paid to its presence in the American prayer book, but also to its lack of requirement. Conversation between priest and people about its history, the teachings of Scripture, whether or not it adds to the beauty of the worship experience, and how it could be done well in a particular space are essential. If, after these conversations, there was a desire for introduction on the highest feast days, a ceremonial practice could be drawn up that was attentive to the ideals of Anglican liturgy (including the importance of the offertory, the balance of the liturgy between word and sacrament, and the role of the people in the consecration of the elements). Done thoughtfully and well, in a conversation among the community, incense is unlikely to provoke as vigorous a response if used in this way—particularly when set alongside of clergy who simply bring it into worship and swing the thurible with as much enthusiasm as they can muster.

APPLYING DEARMER'S IDEALS TO CONTEMPORARY ANGLICAN WORSHIP

Regrettably, rubrical ignorance (or, simply, willful disobedience) still prevails in the church today across all parties in the Episcopal Church. In Dearmer's time he wrote, "But in some mysterious way antiquarianism and clericalism perverted the clergy of all parties and turned them into ruthless innovators."[10] Many priests today still see fit to violate canons and rubrics in the belief that anything that seems right to them is an appropriate prophetic action. Thus,

---

10. Dearmer, *Short Handbook of Public Worship*, 10.

Conclusion—Dearmer Revisited

the people are still held at the whims of their clergy when it comes to what should be simple questions of liturgical practice.

In particular, as the Episcopal Church walks through a period of discernment regarding prayer book revision, attention must be paid to the norms of our worship. There are some in the church who would argue for the greater diversity already found in England, where supplemental liturgical resources are commonly used and the authorized 1662 *Book of Common Prayer* is no longer the common basis for worship.[11] Others disagree strongly, believing that the Anglican ideal of liturgical conformity in one shared prayer book, through which diverse theological perspectives are held together, remains a worthwhile task.[12]

Most significantly, any possible revision will have to deal with the reality in our churches where refusal to follow the rubrics for the reception of communion by the unbaptized continues to be championed in some parishes and even by some bishops. Even small common rubrical violations, like the lack of silence after the fraction, the bringing forward of the bread and wine apart from the alms, the removal of the alms from the altar before the Eucharistic prayer, and the placement of the dismissal, should be considered. Each one of those small violations is not only a violation of the standards of our worship, it results in a theological statement (often unintentional) that runs counter to the goal of the prayer book itself. Conformity to the rubrics—whether of our current prayer book or of the one that may come in the next decade or so—continues to be essential to Anglicanism. It enables us to be united in worship even as we remain diverse in our views. The rubrics give a healthy boundary for a diverse church and ensure the laity have a strong voice in the worship of the church.

The need for a return to a greater emphasis on beauty and art is also essential. In the both the 2012 and 2015 authorized rites of same-sex blessing in the Episcopal Church (the ones that were created anew, not developed from existing prayer book liturgies)

---

11. See, for example, the arguments of Pearson, "Anglican Identity and Common Prayer."

12. See, for example, the responses to Pearson's article by Bauerschmidt et al., "Conformity, Liturgy, and Doctrine."

one of the most significant complaints in social media and other spheres has been that absence of beauty from the liturgy. As quoted earlier, Dearmer wisely wrote, "The bishops have seldom troubled to consult good writers, and have acted as if they thought the art of prose composition was miraculously conferred upon them at their consecration."[13] Substitute the word "liturgical commission" for "bishops" and "formation" for "consecration" and the sentence still fits rather well. As Neil Alexander has argued, if prayer book revision is to go forward, the revision of the language "needs to be done, not by language activists, but by poets, writers, linguists, musicians, and theologians sensitive to the rich complexity of the ways we use words to pray."[14]

Furthermore, Dearmer's insistence upon vestments and ornaments that are well-made is doubly important in our current context of internet shopping and greatly expanded church supply houses, not to mention an increase in homemade vestments that are often a regrettable distraction in the liturgy itself. For churches to endeavor to make their own vestments is something Dearmer would strongly encourage, but care should be taken that they are made well and convey the beauty of the rite in the tradition of the church. Churches would do well to scale back on full sets of paraments, particularly if cost is a concern, and focus on high quality vestments for the clergy and frontals for the altar.

One also hopes that liturgy that is well-done, that highlights the beauty of the rich Anglican tradition, could also serve as an evangelistic tool in our time. We see some of that in places like the Compline Choir at St. Mark's Episcopal Cathedral in Seattle, Washington, where hundreds gather for a beautiful and simple service while thousands more listen online.

When this emphasis on beauty is based upon the Anglican teachings surrounding the sacraments and the incarnation, particularly as Dearmer articulated them, it results in a theologically rich worship experience. However, churches must also return to the ideals of patronage of the arts. In far too many parishes, as budgets

---

13. Dearmer, *Art of Public Worship*, 46–47.
14. Alexander, "Fresh and Familiar," para. 15.

have become tight, music ministries are cut down to the barest possible essentials. Commissioned music and art, which often supported the lives of contemporary artists, is increasingly rare. The church must affirm that beauty and art are avenues of God's revelation, worthy of the support of the worshiping community.

Simple, yet thoughtful, liturgy is another ideal whose time for renewal is long past. Unfortunately, in far too many places simple worship actually means worship that is not well-prepared and thought through. In those places that do prepare well, the level of liturgical fussiness can become a distraction to the worshiping community. And, in our era of liturgical experimentation, worship can sometimes be a jarring experience as the latest idea a priest reads about online is foisted upon the unsuspecting congregation. Technology has certainly increased the availability of a good liturgical sources from history and around the world, but with the modern absence of any curation of that liturgy, each individual priest often becomes the adjudicator of what is good, faithful, beautiful, and edifying to the people—despite the fact that not every priest has been equipped with the training to curate liturgy in that way.

The formation of clergy, particularly in non-seminary contexts, must focus on attention to the rubrics and how to lead liturgy well, in conversation with the people in the congregation. The best and most unobtrusive approaches to vestments, manual actions, and acts of reverence should be honed. Time should not be spent on the creation of experimental liturgies and prayers. Rather, more time should be spent being steeped in the broad and robust tradition of the church, with an emphasis upon the ways in which the rubrics clarify a clergy person's role as a servant of the baptized.

Similar to the questions surrounding incense noted above, I believe it is time for a deeper consideration of question of liturgical position during the celebration of Holy Eucharist. To be clear, I do not believe I have all the answers here—though I do have some strong opinions—and that is why even in my own current cure I continue the practice of celebrating facing the people while at the high altar, instead of returning to the tradition of the priest and people all facing the same direction. However, the questions remain important and the conversations in my own congregation—and in other parts of the church—have been fruitful, even if my own community has not reached the point where we have changed our own normative practice. That said, I do believe that when celebrating facing the people the connection of the priest to the rest of the baptized is often unintentionally ignored or misunderstood—much to the detriment of both priest and people. A conversation surrounding the placement of the priest and the people can heighten an understanding of that connection whether or not a change in practice is made.

All that said, I increasingly wonder if the argument might be made that the importation of the Roman change of liturgical orientation has actually exacerbated the problem of the separation of priest from people in the liturgical act. Dearmer's primary biographer, Donald Gray, suggests that Dearmer would have approved of post-Vatican II developments like celebration *ad populum* (facing the people).[15] Increasingly, however, contemporary liturgical scholars and clergy have noticed that the actual change of focus has moved to the priest's hands and actions during Eucharist rather than the entire community—including the priest—all facing the same direction, towards an altar wherein God becomes present. Dearmer himself believed strongly that eastward-facing celebration helped emphasize the priesthood of all believers and, as noted earlier, even encouraged the clergy present at the celebration to sit facing east.[16]

Furthermore, the celebration of the liturgy facing the people has resulted in two distinct realities that have actually somewhat heightened the clericalism of our liturgies. First, altars were often simply moved out from the wall instead of the entire liturgical space being redesigned. This turned the altar into a stage or place of performance, instead of the original goal of it being the table around which the community gathered.[17] Second, celebration fac-

---

15. Gray, "British Museum Religion," 2.
16. Dearmer, *Parson's Handbook* (12th ed.), 48.
17. No less an advocate of twentieth-century liturgical renewal than Louis Weil argued recently that churches that are unable to redesign their space so that the community gathers around the altar are better off remaining with eastward celebration, rather than creating a situation where the focal point

ing the people has resulted in several common liturgical tics which heighten clericalism and do the opposite of what Dearmer believed was essential, for liturgical movement "to hide the man and to exalt the common priesthood of the Christian congregation."[18] For example, there is the theologically questionable practice of the priest holding up the two halves of the bread after the fraction in an oddly triumphal gesture. This could suggest that Christ is somehow successfully sacrificed once more as opposed to the reality that we have entered mystically into the presence of Christ's sacrifice made once for all time. Further, facing the people has only multiplied the fussiness of the manual actions of the presider in the Eucharistic liturgy, as though their movements are now putting on a show, rather than making visible an ancient prayer.

As I said, my own parish practices celebration *versus populum* at our high altar. This is not a hill upon which any priest should die. At the same time, since the establishment of our side chapel, whose limited space only enables celebration *ad orientem*, even members who once resisted this idea have said that it does feel as though we are all gathered around the altar as a community, facing God together as we ask Christ to become present to us once more.

In the end, regardless of orientation, it is eminently possible to overly clericalize the liturgical action. It is also possible, by doing liturgy carefully and intentionally with contextualization to liturgical space and community practice, to ensure that the liturgy is a celebration of all the people no matter which direction the priest faces. The point here is that prior assumptions about liturgical position seem to be mistaken at times in practice and effect. One must always ask what the underlying ideal is in a liturgical choice and which option actually does further that ideal.

---

of the liturgical space is the priest at the head of the altar; Weil, "Challenges and Possibilities in the Anglican Liturgical Future." See also Shaver, "*O Oriens*: Reassessing Eastward Eucharistic Celebration for Renewed Liturgy," 451–73. Shaver's work was supervised by Weil along with another noted liturgical scholar, Patrick Malloy. For a Roman Catholic analysis of this question, see Lang, *Turning Towards the Lord*.

18. Dearmer, *Parson's Handbook* (12th ed.), 216.

The area of preaching and teaching is one where a revival in contemporary Anglicanism is just as needed now as it was in Dearmer's day. Emphasis upon narrative preaching (which often seems to misunderstand that this homiletical argument was about a narrative *structure* to the sermon and not simply the telling of good stories) has often resulted in preaching that is thin on theology and scripture and only mildly entertaining to the people. Particularly in a post-Christian age such as ours, the catechetical role of good preaching carries renewed importance if we are to equip the people of God fully to take their place in the ministry of the church.

Authenticity in worship remains an issue in our contemporary times. Though the 1979 *Book of Common Prayer* clearly did not envision the use of the General Confession every Sunday,[19] it is such a common practice that on those times it clearly should not be done (for example, in the baptismal liturgy), the people often ask why it was left out. Dearmer's worry that the prevalence of a general confession might replace examination of conscience remains worth considering. The use of it on every day, including the great festal days of the church year, raises questions of authenticity and whether a liturgical choice adequately manifests the theological reality in a festal Eucharistic celebration.[20] Furthermore, the revisions in the trial Marriage liturgies approved in 2015 and again in 2021 must be carried forward into full revision (at least of that rite of the 1979 *Book of Common Prayer*) if our prayer book will bear an authentic relationship to our belief that the sacrament of marriage is open to all couples regardless of gender and sexuality.

While it is unlikely that a return to traditional English altars is necessary, we have already acknowledged that this was not Dearmer's goal. What remains important in contemporary times is to find good and appropriate ways to set off the altar as sacred space, and to do that with without the multiplication of candles and crosses that often distract from the prominence of the altar. Along the same lines, it is unfortunate that clergy have not been as strong

---

19. "On occasion, the Confession may be omitted." *Book of Common Prayer*, 359.

20. See the argument made by Marion J. Hatchett for its omission on great festal days of the church year, *Commentary on the American Prayer Book*, 342.

Conclusion—Dearmer Revisited

in their advocacy for architectural change when it comes to fonts as they have for the moving of altars out from the walls—a fact that would be clear by visiting any diocese and counting altars pulled away from walls in contrast to full immersion fonts. The placement and design of fonts was an even more explicit concern of the 1979 *Book of Common Prayer*, which is explicit that immersion is the preferred form (as it was for Dearmer).

The principle of theologically thoughtful movement is another where a reclamation of Dearmer's ideals are needed. Not only are the movements of too many priests distracting in their exaggeration, but they are often based upon personal preferences instead of upon a careful consideration of the theological implications of their manual actions. This is not only important when it comes to the decision to bow or genuflect, but it relates to the question of when one performs an act of reverence. In the 1979 *Book of Common Prayer*, the final moment of consecration is generally seen as the Great Amen, when the people give their assent to the presider's prayer.[21] To perform an act of reverence at the words of institution is in keeping with ancient custom, but it is essential that the fullest act of reverence should be reserved for the Great Amen, when the Eucharistic Prayer is actually and fully complete.

Though it is unlikely that a return of the three sacred ministers will happen in the majority of parishes anytime soon, far greater thought should be given to what ministers are properly needed in a celebration of Holy Eucharist. Deacons should not be seen as optional additions but, in actuality, celebration of Eucharist without a deacon should be seen as the abnormality. Further, the reclamation of many of the liturgical roles of the sub-deacon, with them instead being performed by what is called a Eucharistic Minister in the current licensing canons of the Episcopal Church, would do much to enhance the role of the laity in the liturgy without merely turning them into mini-priests.

Far too many parishes treat the entry and exit processions as primarily about the long entrance of a choir—something Dearmer strongly resisted. Care must be taken so that it is clear

---

21. Malloy, *Celebrating the Eucharist*, 180–81.

that the procession at the beginning of the liturgy has the altar as its end point and focus and the procession at the end of the liturgy has the movement of the people of God out into the world as its endpoint and focus.

The offertory should be restored to its proper place of dignity in Anglican liturgy, particularly given the rubrics of the current prayer book. The bread, wine, and alms should be brought forward with great solemnity and reverence and all three should remain upon the altar for the duration of the Eucharistic prayer. Ablutions after the prayer of consecration should be reverent and restrained, with the best option being to use chalice veils at that moment and not before the Great Thanksgiving. After all, chalice veils are not pieces of decoration to make the altar look special as the people arrive, as Dearmer notes, but are linens of reverence for consecrated elements.

As our church searches for a theology of confirmation, Dearmer's ideals would call us back to the earlier practice of English Christianity. That is, the chrismation done by the presbyter at baptism, followed by the immediate communion of the baptized, should be a single unified rite of initiation. This had actually been the goal of the original trial rites which led to the *1979 Book of Common Prayer*, "not only were the rites of handlaying and anointing, associated with the gift and seal of the Holy Spirit, added as post-baptismal rites within the rite of baptism itself, but confirmation by a bishop was entirely eliminated."[22] The change was vigorously opposed (especially, unsurprisingly, by the bishops at that time), but the point was made—and the change still needs to be effected. There is no need for a superfluous later confirmation by a bishop and, as noted earlier, history clearly demonstrates that this was yet another importation of a Roman custom upon traditional English liturgy—and one that was strongly resisted for hundreds of years.

Paradoxically, in a day when social justice is very much *en vogue*, there seems to be much less interest in the Christian Socialist insights under which Dearmer worked. For Dearmer was not content merely to argue for liberal politics, and I doubt he would think

---

22. Johnson, *Rites of Christian Initiation*, 411.

Conclusion—Dearmer Revisited

it sufficient to be content with memes on social media or boldy putting a sticker on the bumper of your car. He did not believe it was enough to care for the poor, to provide them with food, shelter, and clothing, but one also needed to advocate for fair labor practices. One needed to stand against systemic injustices that created the circumstances to which the church was seeking to respond. This can be large-scale work, protest, and advocacy—work Dearmer engaged in throughout his life. But it is also bringing the insights of Christian Socialism to bear on the seemingly small decisions of parochial life. For example, when preparing to purchase an item for the church, be it a new set of sanctuary hangings or coffee for the parish hall, attention should be paid to the labor practices behind the item's creation.

Dearmer insisted throughout his life that the church should also invite the poor and working classes into a beautiful experience of the divine through the church's architecture and worship. As he argued then, it remains the case today, that printed service bulletins are a tremendous aid in the unity of the people in worship. While Scripture lessons should not be printed in the bulletin, nor the full text of all prayers (both of these should be primarily aural experiences for the people), bulletins should be arranged simply and in such a way that makes it easy for any person to follow and participate fully. Thoughtfulness with design to ensure they are aesthetically pleasing and also creativity for using them as catechetical tools are essential and possible for parishes of any size. As Dearmer constantly urged, rather than just doing it yourself, clergy should reach out to those with skill and talents in the areas of art and design.

And, of course, renewed attention must be paid to creating a worship experience that truly is transformative, worship that immerses people in an experience of God's love, beauty, and goodness and does the work of changing them even more into the image of that love, beauty, and goodness. As long as our liturgies continue to produce the same grumpy and mean-spirited Christians as every other tradition, we do not have much of an evangelistic message to offer to a divided world. If the people's engagement with Eucharistic liturgy does not enable them better to love their neighbor, then the whole approach must be reconsidered.

Percy Dearmer Revisited

Finally, a renewed sense of humor is just as important in the church today as it was in Dearmer's time. We must never take ourselves—or our opinions—too seriously, lest we forget that we are not saved by the proper practice of our worship but by a generous God who is far more impressed with humility than extravagance.

What might a "prayer book catholic" look like in today's Episcopal Church, in today's Anglican Communion? One hopes that such a priest might bear some resemblance to Percy Dearmer. He is a figure in the church whose influence has been large, though he has often been unfairly treated or ignored by scholars, historians, and theologians alike. By focusing only on questions of riddel posts and appareled amices, too many have missed the importance of his quest for an authentically Anglican expression of worship that falls within the rich tradition and heritage of our church.

Here at the beginning of the twenty-first century, we appear to be entering a new era of possible liturgical revision and reform. The 2015 General Convention of the Episcopal Church directed the Standing Committee on Liturgy and Movement to prepare a plan for the revision of the 1979 *Book of Common Prayer*. The 2018 General Convention's response was a bit confusing to many, rejecting the plans offered, memorializing the 1979 prayer book, and creating the Task Force on Liturgical and Prayer Book Revision. Liturgical resources are being collected, experimentation encouraged, and diocesan task forces being set-up.

In particular, that original call in 2015 for revision and the 2018 resolution which created the task force included this mandate: "utilize the riches of Holy Scripture and our Church's liturgical, cultural, racial, generational, linguistic, gender, physical ability, class and ethnic diversity in order to share common worship."[23] Conversations have now been taking place over the past five years as to what shape this revision should take with most of the energy surrounding a perfection of the work already done and present in the current American prayer book.

---

23. 2015 General Convention, "Resolution A169: Prepare a Plan for Revising the 1979 Book of Common Prayer," 886–87. See also, 2018 General Convention, "A068 Plan for the Revision of the Book of Common Prayer."

Conclusion—Dearmer Revisited

Yet, in the average Episcopal parish, interest in prayer book revision is minor—if it is present at all. Most parishes are instead concerned with how they might grow, how they might be more faithful and vibrant communities of faith. Though debates still persist about weighty questions like the communing of the unbaptized and liturgical marriage equality, many of the debates that framed the 1979 *Book of Common Prayer* have dissipated. Perhaps this means we are in a season where a deeper engagement with, study of, and attention to the rites and rubrics of our prayer book might take place, something that would please Dearmer greatly. Then, drawing from the insights of contemporary liturgical scholarship (especially that which has critiqued and developed some of the original assumptions of the Liturgical Movement) and the richness of our Anglican tradition, a new prayer book might be brought together that can once more call diverse Anglicans together in shared worship.

For Episcopal clergy and lay leaders who seek to revive and renew their parish worship, particularly in today's ecumenical and multicultural context, the rich resources of Percy Dearmer's work provide a wealth of ideals and directions. Though his work does have its limitations, Dearmer's own stated goal was never to encourage every parish to follow the minute recommendations he gave for the fullest possible ceremonial in the English Use. Rather, he was interested in worship that would be authentically and beautifully Anglican. He looked to the sources and riches of the Anglican liturgical tradition and called people in his own time back to those riches, insisting that standards for beauty and social justice must stand side by side.

It is true that a return to the ideals of Dearmer for worship will likely not change the face of the Episcopal Church forever, nor will it evoke another "Decade of Evangelism" (though, given the success of the last one, that is probably a good thing!). Yet, worship well-done in the Anglican tradition does have an evangelistic possibility. As he writes near the end of *The Art of Public Worship*:

> I have no panacea for "filling our churches." We shall not fill the churches yet, for the teeth of the children have been set on edge. Some used to think that they could achieve the desired end by increasing the elaboration of

their ceremonial; but the level refused to rise. Some by diligence in visiting, some by such power of eloquence as is all too rarely found; but the level has refused to rise. A few have become fevered in their disappointment, and think now that novel forms of cultus must at last overcome the indifference; but the level will still refuse to rise. Yet our course is clear and simple. It is to serve God for his own sake: to serve him in spirit and in truth, to worship him in the beauty of holiness and in the holiness of beauty, to give up all that is unreal and insincere, ugly or depressing, tedious, artificial, or mawkish, unsocial, narrow, quarrelsome—not seeking any reward, but because there is a God above us. And in this new way to persevere in a quiet conscience, and therefore with consistent principle, without restlessness or impatience; until gradually the people realize that the church has some better things for them . . . Only if we do what is right, for the sake of the right, all will come right in the end.[24]

Dearmer's words here resonate deeply, even in our own time. Neither the elaboration of rich ceremonial, nor the creation of novel forms of worship, will shift our church. However, if we can serve God for God's own sake, and follow the ideals of Dearmer for Anglican liturgy, we will find a church that is renewed for service—and one that will be well worth inviting people into. This is the task before the Episcopal Church, before Anglicans throughout the Communion, and indeed before all Christians as we face the church of today and seek to be faithful as we bring about the church of tomorrow.

---

24. Dearmer, *Art of Public Worship*, 148.

Bibliography

Alexander, J. Neil. *Celebrating Liturgical Time: Days, Weeks, and Seasons.* New York: Church Publishing, 2014.

———. "Fresh and Familiar." *The Living Church*, November 8, 2016. http://livingchurch.org/covenant/2016/11/08/fresh-and-familiar/.

Anglican Church in Aotearoa, New Zealand. *New Zealand Prayer Book: He Karakia Mihinare O Aotearoa.* Rev. ed. New York: HarperOne, 1997.

Anonymous. "In Memoriam: Percy Dearmer, DD." *Modern Churchman* 26.3 (1936) 114–15.

Bauerschmidt, John, et al. "Conformity, Liturgy, and Doctrine: 3 Responses to Pearson's 'Anglican Identity and Common Prayer.'" *The Living Church*, September 30, 2016. http://livingchurch.org/covenant/2016/09/30/conformity-liturgy-and-doctrine-3-responses-to-pearsons-anglican-identity-and-common-prayer/.

Baxter, Philip. *Sarum Use: The Ancient Customs of Salisbury.* Reading, UK: Spire, 2008.

Bede. *Ecclesiastical History of the English People.* Translated by Leo Sherley-Price and R. E. Latham. London: Penguin, 1990.

———. *Histoire Ecclésiastique de Peuple Anglais: Tome I, Livres I-II.* Sources Chétiennes 489. Edited by André Crépin. Paris: Le Éditions du Cerf, 2005.

Beeson, Trevor. "The Master of Ceremonies: Percy Dearmer, Westminster." In *The Canons: Cathedral Close Encounters*, edited by Trevor Beeson, 98–111. London: Student Christian Movement, 2006.

The Book of Common Prayer and Administration of the Sacraments and Other Rites and Ceremonies of the Church. New York: Church Publishing, 1979.

Bradshaw Paul F., and Maxwell E. Johnson. *The Eucharistic Liturgies: Their Evolution and Interpretation.* Collegeville, MN: Liturgical, 2012.

Chadwick, Owen. *The Mind of the Oxford Movement.* Stanford, CA: Stanford University Press, 1960.

Chamberlain, Jeffrey S. *Accommodating High Churchmen: The Clergy of Sussex 1700–1745.* Chicago: University of Illinois Press, 1997.

Bibliography

Chapman, Mark. *Anglican Theology.* London: T. & T. Clark, 2012.
———. *Anglicanism: A Very Short Introduction.* London: Oxford University Press, 2006.
Cramer, Jared C. *Safeguarded by Glory: Michael Ramsey's Ecclesiology and the Struggles of Contemporary Anglicanism.* Lanham, MD: Lexington, 2010.
Davies, J. G. *The Architectural Setting of Baptism.* London: Barrie & Rockliff, 1962.
Dearmer, Nan. *The Life of Percy Dearmer.* London: Alden, 1940.
Dearmer, Percy. *Art and Religion.* London: Student Christian Movement, 1924.
———. *The Art of Public Worship.* London: Mowbray, 1919.
———. *Body and Soul: An Enquiry into the Effect of Religion Upon Health, with a Description of Christian Works of Healing from the New Testament to the Present Day.* New York: Dutton, 1909.
———. *The Cathedral Church of Oxford: A Description of Its Fabric and a Brief History of the Episcopal See.* London: Bell and Sons, 1899.
———. *The Cathedral Church of Wells: A Description of Its Fabric and a Brief History of the Episcopal See.* London: Bell and Sons, 1899.
———. *Christian Socialism and Practical Christianity.* London: The Clarion, 1897.
———. *Christianity and Art.* New York: Association, 1926.
———. *The Church at Prayer and the World Outside.* London: Clarke, 1923.
———. *Eight Preparations for Communion and the Sanctuary: A Book for Communicants.* London: Society for Promoting Christian Knowledge, 1923.
———. *Everyman's History of the English Church.* London: Mowbray, 1928.
———. *False Gods.* London: Mowbray, 1914.
———. *Fifty Pictures of Gothic Altars: Selected and Described.* London: Green, 1910.
———. *Highways and Byways in Normandy.* London: Macmillan, 1900.
———. *Lessons on the Way: For the Use of Enquirers and Teachers.* 5 vols. London: Society for Promoting of Christian Knowledge, 1926-28.
———. *Linen Ornaments of the Church.* Alcuin Club Tracts 17. London: Mowbray, 1957.
———. *The Necessity of Art.* London: Student Christian Movement, 1924.
———. *The Ornaments of the Ministers.* 2nd ed. London: Mowbray, 1920.
———. "Outward Signs and Inward Light." In *The Fellowship of Silence: Being Experiences in the Common Use of Prayer Without Words*, edited by Cyril Hepher, 165-90. London: MacMillan, 1916.
———. *The Parson's Handbook: Containing Practical Directions both for Parsons and Others as to the Management of the Parish Church and its Services According to the Anglican Use, as Set Forth in the Book of Common Prayer.* 1st ed. London: Richards, 1899. http://anglicanhistory.org/dearmer/handbook/1899/intro.html.
———. *The Parson's Handbook: Containing Practical Directions both for Parsons and Others as to the Management of the Parish Church and Its Services*

BIBLIOGRAPHY

According to the Anglican Use, as Set Forth in the Book of Common Prayer. 12th ed. London: Oxford University Press, 1932.

———. *Patriotism and Fellowship.* London: Murray, 1917.

———. "Preface." In *The Necessity of Art*, v–vii. London: Student Christian Movement, 1924.

———. *The Sanctuary: A Book for Communicants.* London: Rivingtons, 1930.

———. *A Short Handbook of Public Worship in the Churches of the Anglican Communion, for the Clergy, Church Councillors, and the Laity in General.* London: Oxford University Press, 1931.

———. *Some English Altars.* London: Warham Guild, n.d.

———. *The Story of the Prayer Book in the Old and New World and Throughout the Anglican Church.* London: Oxford University Press, 1933.

———. *The Truth about Fasting: With Special Reference to Fasting-Communion.* London: Rivingtons, 1928.

Dearmer, Percy, ed. *The English Hymnal.* Oxford: University Press, 1906.

Dix, Dom Gregory. *The Shape of the Liturgy.* New ed. London: Bloomsbury, 2015.

Fenwick, John R. K., and Bryan D. Spinks. *Worship in Transition: The Liturgical Movement in the Twentieth Century.* New York: Continuum, 1995.

Friedman, Edwin H. *A Failure of Nerve: Leadership in the Age of the Quick Fix.* Edited by Margaret M. Treadwell and Edward W. Beal. New York: Seabury, 2007.

General Convention. "Resolution A169: Prepare a Plan for Revising the 1979 Book of Common Prayer." In *Journal of the General Convention of the Protestant Episcopal Church in the United States of America: Salt Lake City, 2015*, 886–997. New York: General Convention, 2015.

Gray, Donald. "The British Museum Religion: Percy Dearmer in Context." Lecture given to the Anglo-Catholic Historical Society, London, May 8, 2001.

———. "Percy Dearmer." In *They Shaped Our Worship: Essays on Anglican Liturgists*, edited by Christopher Irvine, 71–76. London: Society for Promoting Christian Knowledge, 1998.

———. *Percy Dearmer: A Parson's Pilgrimage.* Norwich: Canterbury, 2000.

Hatchett, Marion J. *Commentary on the American Prayer Book.* New York: Seabury, 1980.

Herring, George. *The Oxford Movement in Practice: The Tractarian Parochial World from the 1830s to the 1870s.* Oxford: University Press, 2016.

James, Gordon P., ed. and trans. *The Origins of the Roman Rite.* Alcuin/GROW Liturgical Study 20. Bramcote: Grove, 1991.

Jeanes, Gordon. "Cranmer and Common Prayer." In *The Oxford Guide to the Book of Common Prayer: A Worldwide Survey*, edited by Charles Hefling and Cynthia Shattuck, 21–38. Oxford: Oxford University Press, 2006.

Johnson, Maxwell E. *The Rites of Christian Initiation: Revised and Expanded Edition.* Collegeville, MN: Liturgical, 2007.

Bibliography

Knight, Frances. *Victorian Christianity at the Fin de Siècle: The Culture of English Religion in a Decadent Age*. London: Tauris, 2016.

Lambert, Malcolm. *Christians and Pagans: The Conversion of Britain from Alban to Bede*. New Haven: Yale University Press, 2010.

Lang, Uwe Michael. *Turning Towards the Lord: Orientation in Liturgical Prayer*. San Francisco: Ignatius, 2009.

Lock, Walter. "The Church." In *Lux Mundi: A Series of Studies in the Religion of the Incarnation*, edited by Charles Gore, 364–402. 2nd ed. London: Murray, 1890.

Luff, Alan. *Strengthen for Service: 100 Years of the English Hymnal*. Norwich: Canterbury, 2005.

Malloy, Patrick. *Celebrating the Eucharist: A Practical Ceremonial Guide for Clergy and Other Liturgical Ministers*. New York: Church Publishing, 2007.

Matthews, Walter Robert. "Introduction." In *The Life of Percy Dearmer*, by Nan Dearmer, 13–15. London: Alden, 1940.

Memorial Services: Extracted by Permission from "A Prayer-Book Revised" as Issued in 1913 with a Preface from the Bishop of Oxford. Alcuin Prayer Book Revision Pamphlets VI. Oxford: Mowbry, 1914.

Newman, James. "To Creed or Not To Creed: That Is the Question. On the History and Usage of the Nicene Creed—A Fresh Evaluation." Paper presented at The Madres & the Padres Clergy Study Group, Los Angeles, California, November, 2011. https://anglicanism.org/to-creed-or-not-to-creed-that-is-the-question.

Nockles, Peter B. *The Oxford Movement in Context: Anglican High Churchmanship 1760–1857*. Cambridge: University Press, 1997.

Pearson, Andrew. "Anglican Identity and Common Prayer." *Living Church*, September 26, 2016. http://livingchurch.org/covenant/2016/09/26/anglican-identity-and-common-prayer/.

Rowell, Geoffrey. *The Vision Glorious: Themes and Personalities of the Catholic Revival of Anglicanism*. Oxford: Oxford University Press, 1983.

Shaver, Stephen R. "*O Oriens*: Reassessing Eastward Eucharistic Celebration for Renewed Liturgy." *Anglican Theological Review* 94.3 (Summer 2012) 451–73.

Spencer, Stephen. *The SCM Studyguide to Anglicanism*. London: Student Christian Movement, 2010.

Spinks, Bryan. "The Prayer Book 'Crisis' in England." In *The Oxford Guide to the Book of Common Prayer: A Worldwide Survey*, edited by Charles Hefling and Cynthia Shattuck, 239–43. Oxford: Oxford University Press, 2006.

Stelten, Leo F. *Dictionary of Ecclesiastical Latin: With an Appendix of Latin Expressions Defined and Clarified*. Peabody, MA: Hendrickson, 1995.

Stevick, Daniel B. "Canon Law." In *The Study of Anglicanism*, edited by Stephen Sykes et al., 216–45. Rev. ed. London: Society for Promoting Christian Knowledge, 1999.

Turrell, James F. *Celebrating the Rites of Initiation: A Practical Guide for Clergy and Other Liturgical Ministers*. New York: Church Publishing, 2013.

Bibliography

Warner, George F., ed. *The Stowe Missal: Volume II*. London: Harrison & Sons, 1915.

Weil, Louis. "Challenges and Possibilities in the Anglican Liturgical Future." Lecture, Advanced Degrees Program. Sewanee, TN. June 18, 2016.

Wilkinson, Richard William. "A History of Hymns Ancient and Modern." PhD thesis, University of Hull, 1985. https://hydra.hull.ac.uk/assets/hull:8304a/content.

Williams, Hugh. *Christianity in Early Britain*. Oxford: Clarendon, 1912.

———. *Gildas: The Ruin of Britain, Fragments from Lost Letters, The Penitential, Together with the Lorica of Gildas*. London: Cymmrodorion, 1899.

Williams, Scott. *Church Diversity: Sunday, the Most Segregated Day of the Week*. Green Forest, AR: New Leaf, 2011.

Yates, Nigel. *Anglican Ritualism in Victorian Britain: 1830–1910*. Oxford: Oxford University Press, 1999.

Index

ad orientem, 13, 74, 95–97
Adderly, James, 19
alb, 29, 31, 44, 45, 67, 77,
Alcuin Club, 53–54
Alexander, J. Neil, x, 1, 35, 94, 105
altar, 7, 13, 18, 26–28, 37, 41,
    45, 70, 74, 78–81, 84, 91,
    93–100,
amice, xiii, 102
anaphora, 37
Anglican Communion, xiv–xv, 102,
Anglo-Catholic, 13, 16–17, 25,
    54, 107
apparels, xiii, 102
architecture, xi, 1, 4, 16, 20, 25–26,
    33, 76, 79, 99, 101, 106
art, 1–4, 9, 16, 18, 25–26, 30, 40,
    45–46, 50, 61–67, 71, 74,
    77, 81, 93–95, 101, 103,
    106, 107
Augustine of Canterbury, 38, 82

baptism, 1, 38, 64, 68, 69, 72, 79,
    82–84, 88, 98, 100
beauty, x, ix, xi, xi–xii, 2, 5, 18–19,
    22, 40, 50, 53–54, 61–67,
    70, 91–95, 101, 103–104
Bede, 83–84
Bernard of Clairvaux, 62

bishops. *See* episcopate
Blomfield, Charles, 40
Book of Common Prayer, v, 11–12,
    14, 20–21, 32, 36, 40–41,
    44–46, 48–49, 54, 57, 61,
    69–70, 74–75, 77, 80, 91, 93,
    98–99, 102–103, 105–108
Briggs, Henry, 6
Brightman, Frank Edward, 20
"British Museum Religion," 3–4,
    19–21
Buddhism, 64

candles, 7, 13–14, 20, 30, 39, 41,
    51, 69–70, 98
capitalism, 17
cassock, 21, 76–77, 84
catechesis, 75, 98, 101
celtic christianity, 37–39
ceremonial, 7, 11–12, 15, 38, 41,
    50–51, 57–59, 66, 68, 70–
    71, 80–81, 92, 103–104
Charles II, 42
chasuble, 43, 45, 47, 53
Chesterton, G.K., 21
choirs, 35, 53, 67, 69, 71, 76–77,
    81, 94, 99
Christian Social Union, 5, 17

111

Index

Christian Socialism, 2, 3, 5–6, 9, 17–18, 22, 101
church fathers, 10, 64
ciboria, 26, 78
City Temple, 29
clerk, 2, 47, 81, 86
communion, 13, 15, 20, 27, 41, 44, 46, 68, 72, 75–76, 82, 88, 93, 100, 102, 104
confession, 77, 98
confirmation, 28, 35, 82–83, 89, 100
cope, 44, 53
cotta, 53, 67
creeds, 29, 34–35, 66, 80, 90
Cromwell, Oliver, 60
curtains, dorsal, xiii, 26
curtains, side, 7, 26

dalmatic, 47, 72
Davidson, Randall, 4
deacon, 47, 73, 91, 99
decalogue, 78
Dickens, Charles, 3
Dix, Dom Gregory, 37

eastern christianity, 37, 39, 46, 51
eastward facing, see *ad orientem*
ecumenism, xiii–xiv, 32, 34, 57, 89, 90, 103
Edward VI, 41–43, 47, 52
English Hymnal, The, 17, 24–25,
English Use, xiii, xv–xvi, 16, 32, 55, 89, 103
Episcopal Church, xi, 27, 34, 42, 88, 92–93, 99, 102–103
episcopate, 10, 13–15, 39–40, 42, 47, 58, 65, 73, 79, 83–84, 93, 94, 100
eucharist, xi, 16, 19–20, 37–40, 46, 51, 59, 70, 81–82, 88, 90, 93, 95–101
evangelical, 2, 4, 6, 9, 12, 44, 53, 55, 90
evangelistic, 59, 63, 94, 101, 103

fasting communion, 15, 75, 107
font, baptismal, 38, 79, 81, 99
Frere, Walter Howard, xv, 20
Friedman, Edwin, 87
frontal, 69, 94

gallican, 37–39
genuflection, 20, 80, 99
Gore, Charles, 4, 6, 16–17, 53–54
gothic, 13, 26, 50, 85
gregorian chant. *See* plainsong chant
Guild of St. Matthew, 15, 17–18

Hatchett, Marion, 21, 98
Headlam, Stewart, 15, 17
Henry VIII, 43
High Church, 6–7, 9–10, 15, 40, 45, 47, 58
Housman, Laurence, 25
hymnody, 24–25, 50–51, 66
Hymns Ancient and Modern, 24–25

immersion, 84, 99
incarnation, 15–16, 64, 66, 80, 94
incense, 14, 90–92, 95

Jerome, 83
Justin Martyr, 20

Keble, John, 20

Latimer, Hugh, 21
laudian, xiii, 40
Littledale, Richard, 43
liturgical colors, 4–5, 27, 48, 72, 82
Liturgical Movement, 22, 70, 84, 97, 103
lord's table. *See* altar
Low Church, 36, 44, 47, 62
Lutheran, 54
Lux Mundi movement, 15–16, 64

manual actions, 82, 95, 97, 99

INDEX

Maurice, F.D., 17
medieval. *See* middle ages
middle ages, 20, 26, 34, 36, 41, 47, 50–51, 59, 62, 68, 78, 91
Milton, John, 60
moderation, 11, 15, 17, 43, 51, 54, 71, 91
Morris, William, 4–6
music, xv, 6–7, 9, 16, 24–25, 33, 51, 63, 66–67, 71, 94–95
musician, 3, 66, 94

Neal, John Mason, xv
Newman, John Henry, 12, 40
Norris, William Foxley, 8

offertory, 37, 46, 82, 92, 100
ornaments, 2, 18, 40–44, 51, 53, 67, 71, 85
Ornaments Rubric, 40–44, 48, 88
Oxford Movement, 1, 9–15, 22, 40

parliament, 41, 43, 74
Phillpotts, Henry, 40
plainsong chant, 6, 8, 25, 34, 75
Poore, Richard, 49
Powell, York, 2, 4, 17
prayer book revision, 49, 53–54, 93–94, 98, 102
procession, 81, 99–100
proprietary chapel, 6
pulpit, 18, 74, 86
Puritans, 42, 47, 52, 62, 64, 79

Quakers. *See* Society of Friends

Reformation, 1, 4, 10, 45, 49, 58, 69, 73, 80
riddel posts, xiii, 26, 78, 79, 102
Ritualism, xv, 1, 2, 9, 11–19, 21–22, 40, 43–44, 46, 58, 63, 68, 70–71, 74–75, 81
Roman [Catholic], xiii, 2, 6, 11–12, 16, 21, 36–40, 43–48, 50–51, 55, 62, 67–68, 70–73, 81, 83–84, 91, 96–97, 100
Roman Rite, 6, 37, 39
rood, 79, 81
rubrics, 12, 14, 21, 40–44, 47–49, 52–53, 57–59, 75, 79–80, 82, 88, 92–93, 95, 100, 103
Ruskin, John, 4, 77

sacrament, 7, 15–16, 27, 32, 46, 65, 80, 89, 92, 94, 98
Salisbury Cathedral, 43, 48–49
same-sex marriage, 93, 103
Sarum, 1, 20, 39, 47–49
Savoy Conference, 42
Shepherd, Massey, xv
Society of Friends, 29, 61, 89
Songs of Praise, 25
St. Mary's, Primrose Hill, 6–9, 24–25, 29, 61
stained glass, 26, 35, 50
Strong, Thomas Banks, 1
sub-deacon, 47, 81, 99
surplice, 18, 42, 44, 47, 53, 67, 71, 76, 84
sweatshops, 18, 67, 84

Temple, Frederick, 7
Temple, William, 8
tippet, 21
tractarianism, 6, 9–15, 18, 22, 75–76

Vatican II, xiv, 96
veil, chalice, 72–73, 82, 100
vestments, xi, 2, 12–14, 27–28, 41–42, 44, 46–47, 51, 53, 67, 69, 72, 74, 77, 84, 86, 94–95
via media, xiv, 11
Victorian, 52–53, 57, 72
Ward, William George, 40
Wesley, John, 76
Westminster Abbey, 8
Williams, Ralph Vaughan, 25

www.ingramcontent.com/pod-product-compliance
Lightning Source LLC
Chambersburg PA
CBHW050837160426
43192CB00011B/2060